THE KITCHEN LIBRARY

FAVOURITES

THE KITCHEN LIBRARY
TEATIME FAVOURITES

Brian Binns

OCTOPUS BOOKS

CONTENTS

This edition published 1988 by
Octopus Books Limited
Michelin House
81 Fulham Road
London SW3 6RB

Reprinted 1988

© Cathay Books 1983
ISBN 0 7064 3244 4

Printed by Mandarin Offset in Hong Kong

NOTES

Standard spoon measures are used in all recipes
1 tablespoon=one 15 ml spoon
1 teaspoon=one 5 ml spoon
All spoon measures are level.

For all recipes, quantities are given in both metric
and imperial measures. Follow either set but not a
mixture of both, because they are not
interchangeable.

Eggs used in the recipes are standard size, i.e. size
3, unless otherwise stated. If large eggs are
specified, use size 1.

If fresh yeast is unobtainable, substitute dried yeast
but use only half the recommended quantity and
follow the manufacturer's instructions for
reconstituting.

Recipes for basic pastries and cake fillings (marked
with an asterisk) are given in the reference section
(pages 90-93). Adjust the amount as required by
increasing or decreasing the basic quantities in
proportion.

INTRODUCTION

This collection of cakes and bakes contains traditional favourites dating back to Victorian times as well as new ideas and variations. Traditional recipes can be found in the yeast section and are well worth the extra time involved. In contrast, there's a selection of cakes from other countries for you to try, as well as a few delicious gâteaux and torten for that rather special teatime gathering; they could, of course, equally well be served as desserts. Something savoury is also often appreciated at teatime and the selection of finger foods is sure to please; they could also be served at an early evening drinks gathering. Whatever your family's tastes in cakes – plain or fancy, fruity or spicy – there's something here for them all. You'll enjoy cooking them, too.

SMALL CAKES & BISCUITS

Queen Cakes

125 g (4 oz) caster
   sugar
finely grated rind of
   1 lemon
125 g (4 oz) butter,
   softened
2 eggs, beaten
125 g (4 oz)
   self-raising flour
50 g (2 oz) sultanas
25 g (1 oz) currants
2 tablespoons milk
8 glacé cherries,
   halved (optional)
icing sugar, sifted,
   for sprinkling

Cream together the sugar, lemon rind and butter until light and fluffy. Add the eggs a little at a time, beating well after each addition.

Sift the flour onto the mixture and fold in gently, then fold in the fruit and milk. Spoon into 15 well buttered queen cake tins or bun tins; if liked, place half a cherry in each tin first.

Bake in a preheated moderately hot oven, 190°C (375°F), Gas Mark 5, for 10 to 12 minutes or until just firm to touch. Leave in the tins for 15 minutes, then invert onto a wire rack to cool. Dust lightly with icing sugar to serve.

Makes 15

NOTE: Queen cake tins are fluted, in various attractive shapes.

Brown Sugar Meringues

3 egg whites
75 g (3 oz) caster
   sugar
125 g (4 oz) soft
   brown sugar
142 ml (¼ pint)
   whipping or
   double cream,
   whipped

Whisk the egg whites until soft peaks form, then gradually whisk in the caster sugar until the mixture forms firm peaks. Sprinkle the brown sugar over the mixture and fold in carefully.

Place tablespoons of the meringue on a baking sheet lined with non-stick paper, spacing well apart, to make 10 to 12 meringue halves.

Bake in a preheated cool oven, 140°C (275°F), Gas Mark 1, for 1½ hours; leave in the oven until the oven is completely cold. Carefully remove the meringues from the baking sheet, using a palette knife.

Carefully and gently break each flat base to form a cavity. Fill this with cream and sandwich the meringue halves together in pairs.
Makes 5 or 6

Sponge Drops

Speed and gentleness are essential, as this very light mixture quickly loses its volume if handled heavily or left to stand. Have all ingredients at room temperature. Leave the sponges for 2 hours after filling – they become softer and more delicious.

3 eggs
125 g (4 oz) caster
    sugar
125 g (4 oz) plain
    flour, sifted
TO FINISH:
25 g (1 oz) caster
    sugar
2 tablespoons
    raspberry jam
284 ml (½ pint)
    double cream,
    whipped

Whisk the eggs and sugar together until pale and thick. Gently fold in the flour.

Place the mixture in a piping bag fitted with a 1 cm (½ inch) plain nozzle. Pipe into discs, 3.5 cm (1½ inches) in diameter, onto lined baking sheets, 5 cm (2 inches) apart; there should be enough for about 48 discs. Sift a little sugar over them and bake in a preheated moderately hot oven, 190°C (375°F), Gas Mark 5, for 10 minutes or until light golden brown. Cool on the baking sheets.

When cold, dampen the underside of the lining paper and carefully peel off the discs. Sandwich together in pairs with jam and cream.
Makes about 24

Bolton Flat Cakes

250 g (8 oz)
    self-raising flour
½ teaspoon salt
75 g (3 oz) lard
4 tablespoons milk
250 g (8 oz) jam
milk to glaze

Sift the flour and salt into a bowl and rub in the lard until the mixture resembles breadcrumbs. Add the milk; mix to a smooth dough. Divide into two 125 g (4 oz) pieces and two 65 g (2½ oz) pieces. Shape into balls, cover and leave for 5 minutes.

Roll out the two largest pieces on a floured surface into 20 cm (8 inch) rounds and spread with jam, leaving a 1 cm (½ inch) border; dampen the border.

Roll out the two remaining pieces into 18 cm (7 inch) rounds and lay them carefully on top, turning the edge of the larger round in to seal the rounds together. Place on greased baking sheets, smooth side up, prick with a fork and brush with milk.

Bake in a preheated moderately hot oven, 190°C (375°F), Gas Mark 5, for 20 minutes or until pale golden. Serve slightly warm or cold, spread with butter and cut into triangles.
Makes two 20 cm (8 inch) rounds

Ginger Buns

125 g (4 oz)
  margarine
125 g (4 oz) soft
  brown sugar
2 eggs
125 g (4 oz) golden
  syrup
175 g (6 oz)
  self-raising flour
3 teaspoons ground
  ginger
1 teaspoon ground
  mixed spice
1 tablespoon milk
TO FINISH:
150 g (5 oz) icing
  sugar, sifted
3-4 pieces preserved
  ginger, sliced

Cream the margarine and sugar together until light and fluffy. Add the eggs one at a time, beating well after each addition. Beat in the syrup.

Sift the flour and spices onto the mixture and mix well. Add the milk and continue mixing until smooth. Spoon into 24 greased and floured bun tins, until about three-quarters full.

Bake in a preheated moderately hot oven, 190°C (375°F), Gas Mark 5, for 12 minutes until just firm to the touch. Cool on a wire rack.

To finish, mix the icing sugar with a little water to make a smooth icing. Place a teaspoon of icing on each bun and top with a slice of ginger.
Makes 24

American Muffins

This is a rather well anglicized version. The Americans would replace butter with margarine or shortening, and blueberries would replace blackcurrants.

1 egg
90 ml (3 fl oz) milk
75 g (3 oz) butter,
  softened
75 g (3 oz) sugar
3 teaspoons baking
  powder
150 g (5 oz) plain
  flour, sifted
75 g (3 oz) frozen
  blackcurrants,
  partially thawed
TOPPING:
25 g (1 oz) sugar
1 teaspoon ground
  cinnamon

Whisk the egg and milk together. Beat in the softened butter.

Mix the sugar, baking powder and flour together and stir into the mixture. Stir thoroughly until smooth, then add the blackcurrants, folding them in gently to avoid breaking, until evenly distributed.

Spoon the mixture into 15 greased and floured deep bun tins, until about three-quarters full. Mix the topping ingredients together and sprinkle over the muffin mixture.

Bake in a preheated moderate oven, 180°C (350°F), Gas Mark 4, for 20 minutes until firm to the touch. Cool on a wire rack. These muffins are best eaten very fresh.
Makes 15

Dairy Cream Curls

2 eggs
50 g (2 oz) caster
  sugar
50 g (2 oz) plain
  flour, sifted
TO FINISH:
12 teaspoons
  raspberry jam
142 ml (¼ pint)
  double or
  whipping cream,
  whipped
icing sugar, sifted,
  for sprinkling

Whisk the eggs and sugar together until the mixture is light and the whisk leaves a trail. Fold in the flour.

Drop tablespoons of the mixture onto a lined baking sheet, spacing well apart and keeping them oval in shape.

Bake in a preheated hot oven, 220°C (425°F), Gas Mark 7, for 7 minutes or until pale golden and springy to touch. Cool on the baking sheet.

As soon as the sponge ovals are cold, dampen the underside of the paper and peel away. Spread the jam on the flat side of the cakes and pipe or spoon cream across the centre.

Fold in half and dust lightly with icing sugar. Serve immediately.

Makes 12

Langue de Chat Biscuits

50 g (2 oz) icing
 sugar, sifted
60 ml (2 fl oz)
 whipping cream
50 g (2 oz) plain
 flour, sifted
few drops of vanilla
 essence
1 egg white, stiffly
 whisked

Mix the icing sugar and cream together, then stir in the flour to make a smooth paste. Fold in vanilla essence to taste and the egg white.

Place in a piping bag fitted with a 5 mm (¼ inch) plain nozzle and pipe 7.5 cm (3 inch) lengths on greased and floured baking sheets.

Bake in a preheated moderately hot oven, 200°C (400°F), Gas Mark 6, for 12 to 15 minutes, until the edges are golden brown. Cool on a wire rack.

Makes about 25

Oatmeal Crunchies

250 g (8 oz)
 self-raising flour,
 sifted
50 g (2 oz) porridge
 oats
75 g (3 oz)
 granulated sugar
75 g (3 oz) soft
 brown sugar
¼ teaspoon salt
125 g (4 oz) butter
3 teaspoons golden
 syrup
2 tablespoons milk

Put the flour, oats, sugars and salt in a bowl and mix well. Rub in the butter to form a crumble consistency. Mix the syrup and milk together, add to the dry ingredients and mix to a stiff dough. Knead lightly and shape into a roll, 5 cm (2 inches) in diameter. Chill for about 1 hour until very firm, then cut into 5 mm (¼ inch) thick slices. Place on greased baking sheets, 1 cm (½ inch) apart.

Bake in a preheated moderately hot oven, 190°C (375°F), Gas Mark 5, for 15 minutes. Leave on the baking sheet for 1 minute, then transfer to a wire rack to cool.

Makes 30

Flapjacks

175 g (6 oz) butter
25 g (1 oz) golden
 syrup
125 g (4 oz) soft
 brown sugar
250 g (8 oz)
 porridge oats
50 g (2 oz)
 desiccated coconut

Melt the butter and syrup together in a pan. Remove from the heat and stir in the remaining ingredients. Turn into a greased 18 × 28 cm (7 × 11 inch) Swiss roll tin and spread evenly.

Bake in a preheated moderate oven, 180°C (350°F), Gas Mark 4, for 15 minutes. Cool slightly, then cut into fingers and remove from the tin.

Makes 22

Ginger Nuts

Once you have made these you will never want to buy them again – they are so simple and really delicious.

250 g (8 oz) self-raising flour
1 tablespoon ground ginger, or to taste
75 g (3 oz) margarine
125 g (4 oz) golden syrup
125 g (4 oz) demerara sugar
2 tablespoons milk

Sift the flour and ginger together into a large bowl. Add the margarine and rub in very finely.

Mix the syrup, sugar and milk together, add to the flour mixture and mix to a smooth dough. Knead lightly and shape into a roll, about 3.5 cm (1½ inches) in diameter. Chill for about 1 hour until the mixture is stiff enough to slice. Cut into 5 mm (¼ inch) thick slices and place on greased baking sheets, about 1 cm (½ inch) apart.

Bake in a preheated moderate oven, 180°C (350°F), Gas Mark 4, for about 20 minutes until the tops are cracked and golden brown. Leave on the baking sheet for 1 minute, then transfer to a wire rack to cool.

Makes about 36

NOTE: The dough roll can be kept in the refrigerator for several days.

Almond Shortbreads

200 g (7 oz) plain flour, sifted
50 g (2 oz) ground almonds
125 g (4 oz) caster sugar
175 g (6 oz) butter, softened
24 split almonds

Put the flour, ground almonds, sugar and butter in a bowl and mix together to form a smooth dough. Shape into a rectangular log, 15 cm (6 inches) long, 7.5 cm (3 inches) wide and 3 cm (1¼ inches) high. Chill for at least 1 hour.

Cut into slices approximately 5 mm (¼ inch) thick and place well apart on baking sheets. Press a split almond into the centre of each and bake in a preheated cool oven, 140°C (275°F), Gas Mark 1, for 30 to 35 minutes, until pale golden. Cool on a wire rack.

Makes 24

Coconut Macaroons

250 g (8 oz)
   desiccated coconut
300 g (10 oz) sugar
5 egg whites
50 g (2 oz) glacé
   cherries, halved

Mix the coconut, sugar and egg whites together in a saucepan. Heat gently, stirring carefully with a wooden spoon, until the mixture is warm but not hot – about 60°C (120°F). Remove from the heat and leave until cold.

Divide the mixture into 18 mounds on a greased and floured baking sheet. Top each mound with half a glacé cherry and bake in a preheated moderate oven, 180°C (350°F), Gas Mark 4, for 20 minutes or until pale golden brown. Cool on a wire rack.
Makes 18

TARTS & PASTRIES

Honey and Almond Tarts

These are delicious – soft, nutty toffee in a melting case.

250 g (8 oz) sweet
  short pastry*
50 g (2 oz) butter
50 g (2 oz) sugar
50 g (2 oz) clear
  honey
75 g (3 oz) flaked
  almonds
1 tablespoon double
  cream

Roll out the pastry thinly on a floured surface and use to line eighteen 6 cm (2½ inch) patty tins. Place the butter, sugar and honey in a heavy-based pan and heat gently until melted. Bring to the boil, then remove from the heat and stir in the almonds and cream. Leave until cold, then divide between the pastry cases.

Bake in a preheated moderately hot oven, 200°C (400°F), Gas Mark 6, for 20 minutes. Cool on a wire rack.

Makes 18

Yorkshire Curd Tarts

250 g (8 oz) short
  flan pastry*
50 g (2 oz) butter,
  softened
50 g (2 oz) caster
  sugar
½ teaspoon ground
  nutmeg
2 tablespoons fresh
  white breadcrumbs
2 eggs, lightly beaten
227 g (8 oz) curd
  cheese, sieved
juice of ½ lemon
50 g (2 oz) currants

Roll out the pastry thinly on a floured surface and use to line eighteen 6 cm (2½ inch) tartlet tins.

Mix together the butter, sugar, nutmeg and breadcrumbs. Stir in the eggs and cheese, mixing well. Finally stir in the lemon juice and currants.

Divide the mixture between the pastry cases and bake in a preheated moderately hot oven, 190°C (375°F), Gas Mark 5, for 20 to 25 minutes until the filling is set. Cool on a wire rack.

Makes 18

VARIATION: This recipe could also be used to make one 20 cm (8 inch) flan.

Lemon Tarts

175 g (6 oz) short
  flan pastry*
1 egg
50 g (2 oz) caster
  sugar
50 g (2 oz) butter
15 g (½ oz) ground
  almonds
finely grated rind of
  1 lemon

Roll out the pastry thinly on a floured surface and use to line twelve 6 cm (2½ inch) tartlet tins.

Put the egg and sugar in a bowl; stir with a fork until evenly mixed but not aerated. Warm butter until just melted, then stir into the egg mixture. Stir in the almonds and lemon rind.

Three-quarters fill the pastry cases with the mixture and bake in a preheated moderately hot oven, 190°C (375°F), Gas Mark 5, for about 15 minutes, until golden brown. Cool on a wire rack.

Makes 12

VARIATION: Top with a thin glacé icing made with icing sugar and lemon juice.

Coconut and Orange Tarts

Bitter-sweet and nutty – these are rather special.

175 g (6 oz) sweet
  short pastry*
75 g (3 oz) caster
  sugar
75 g (3 oz)
  desiccated coconut
1 egg, beaten
1½ tablespoons
  orange marmalade
finely grated rind of
  1 orange

Roll out the pastry thinly on a floured surface and use to line twelve 6 cm (2½ inch) patty tins.

Place the remaining ingredients in a bowl and mix well together. Divide the mixture evenly between the pastry cases and bake in a preheated moderately hot oven, 190°C (375°F), Gas Mark 5, for 20 minutes until golden. Cool on a wire rack.

Makes 12

Syrup Tarts

125 g (4 oz) sweet
  short pastry*
40 g (1½ oz) fresh
  white breadcrumbs
4 tablespoons golden
  syrup, warmed
1 tablespoon lemon
  juice

Roll out the pastry thinly on a floured surface and use to line ten 6 cm (2½ inch) patty tins.

Mix together the breadcrumbs, syrup and lemon juice. Divide the mixture between the pastry cases and bake in a preheated moderately hot oven, 200°C (400°F), Gas Mark 6, for 20 minutes. Cool on a wire rack. Serve warm or cold.

Makes 10

Maids of Honour

125 g (4 oz) easy
  flaky pastry* or
  puff pastry*
40 g (1½ oz) butter,
  softened
50 g (2 oz) caster
  sugar
finely grated rind of
  1 lemon
1 egg, lightly beaten
50 g (2 oz) ground
  almonds
1 tablespoon double
  cream
3 teaspoons raspberry
  jam

Roll out the pastry thinly on a floured surface and prick all over with a fork. Use to line twelve 6 cm (2½ inch) tartlet tins.

Mix the butter and sugar together, without beating. Add the lemon rind and egg, then the almonds and cream. Stir gently until smooth.

Place about ¼ teaspoon jam in each pastry case. Cover with the filling to three-quarters fill the cases.

Bake in a preheated moderately hot oven, 190°C (375°F), Gas Mark 5, for 15 to 20 minutes or until golden brown. Cool on a wire rack.

Makes 12

Congress Tarts

175 g (6 oz) easy flaky pastry*
5 teaspoons raspberry jam
75 g (3 oz) ground almonds
175 g (6 oz) caster sugar
3 egg whites

Roll out the pastry thinly on a floured surface, prick well with a fork and use to line eighteen 6 cm (2½ inch) tartlet tins. Reserve the pastry trimmings. Put ¼ teaspoon jam into each pastry case.

Mix the ground almonds and sugar together, add the egg whites and beat well with a wooden spoon for about 3 minutes; the mixture should be the consistency of thick cream. Drop ½ tablespoon into each pastry case – it should run smoothly and three-quarters fill the case.

Cut pastry trimmings into strips, 5 mm (¼ inch) × 6 cm (2½ inches). Place them crosswise on top of the filling. Leave to stand for 1 hour.

Bake in a preheated moderate oven, 180°C (350°F), Gas Mark 4, for 25 minutes, until golden. Cool on a wire rack.

Makes 18

Apple Crescents

175 g (6 oz) puff
    pastry*, or use a
    212 g (7½ oz)
    packet frozen puff
    pastry, thawed
300 g (10 oz)
    cooking apple,
    peeled, cored and
    finely diced
1 tablespoon caster
    sugar
TO FINISH:
caster sugar
200 ml (⅓ pint)
    whipping or
    double cream,
    whipped

Roll out the pastry on a floured
surface to a 3 mm (⅛ inch) thickness.
Cut out as many 10 cm (4 inch)
rounds as possible. Press trimmings
together and roll out again, cutting
out more 10 cm (4 inch) rounds; this
second rolling will not rise quite as
well. Roll the rounds a little across the
centre to make them slightly oval.

Mix the apple and sugar together,
and place a tablespoon of the mixture
in the centre of each pastry round.
Dampen the edges with water and
fold to make half moons, enclosing
the apple; seal edges. Brush lightly
with water and sprinkle with sugar.

Place on baking sheets and bake in
a preheated hot oven, 220°C (425°F),
Gas Mark 7, for 15 minutes or until
golden brown. Transfer to a wire
rack and leave until cold. Carefully
split the crescents along the join and
pipe in whipped cream.
Makes about 10

Eccles Cakes

175 g (6 oz) easy
  flaky* or puff
  pastry*
25 g (1 oz) sugar
FILLING:
125 g (4 oz) currants
25 g (1 oz) demerara
  sugar
25 g (1 oz) butter,
  melted

Roll out the pastry on a floured surface to a 3 mm (⅛ inch) thickness and cut out as many 10 cm (4 inch) rounds as possible.

Mix the filling ingredients together and place a heaped teaspoon of the mixture in the middle of the pastry rounds. Fold the edges in towards the centre, pinch them together and flatten slightly. Fit each round in a 6 cm (2½ inch) pastry cutter and flatten to the size of the cutter, forming a neat round shape. Make 3 small cuts in the top of each one.

Brush the tops lightly with water and dip into the sugar. Place on a baking sheet and bake in a preheated hot oven, 220°C (425°F), Gas Mark 7, for 15 to 20 minutes or until golden brown. Cool on a wire rack.

Makes about 10

Vanilla Slices

175 g (6 oz) puff
pastry*, or use a
212 g (7½ oz)
packet frozen puff
pastry, thawed
CUSTARD:
40 g (1½ oz)
cornflour
600 ml (1 pint) milk
125 g (4 oz) sugar
2 eggs, lightly beaten
few drops vanilla
essence
25 g (1 oz) butter
(preferably
unsalted)
ICING:
150 g (5 oz) icing
sugar, sifted
3-4 teaspoons water
few drops of food
colouring

Roll out pastry on a floured surface to a 35 × 18 cm (14 × 8 inch) rectangle and cut into 2 strips, 9 cm (4 inches) wide. Prick deeply all over. Place on a baking sheet and bake in a preheated moderately hot oven, 190°C (375°F), Gas Mark 5, for 25 minutes or until crisp. Trim edges with a sharp knife and leave on the baking sheet to cool.

Meanwhile, make the custard. Mix the cornflour to a thin paste with a little of the milk in a basin. Place the remaining milk and the sugar in a pan and bring to the boil. Pour onto the blended cornflour, stirring constantly with a whisk. Return to the pan and bring to the boil, stirring constantly until thick and smooth. Remove from the heat and whisk in the eggs and vanilla essence to taste. Dot the butter over the surface; it will simply melt and form a thin film over the top, which will stop a skin forming.

Mix the icing sugar with enough water to make a smooth coating icing. Transfer 2 tablespoons to a small bowl and mix in a few drops of colouring. Spread the plain icing on top of one pastry strip. Put the coloured icing in a piping bag fitted with a writing nozzle and pipe parallel lines across the plain icing at 5 mm (¼ inch) intervals. Draw a cocktail stick across the lines to create a marbled effect.

Stir the slightly warm custard to incorporate the melted butter and spread on the underside of the other pastry strip, just along the centre.

Carefully position the iced pastry strip on top and press gently. Leave until completely cold then, using a sharp knife, cut into slices.

Makes 8
VARIATION: Replace custard with jam and whipped cream. Make icing with coffee essence instead of water.

Almond Slices

350 g (12 oz) short
    flan pastry*
50 g (2 oz)
    raspberry jam
250 g (8 oz) caster
    sugar
175 g (6 oz) ground
    almonds
25 g (1 oz) ground
    rice
3 eggs, lightly beaten
25 g (1 oz) flaked
    almonds

Roll out the pastry thinly on a floured surface and use to line an 18 × 28 cm (7 × 11 inch) Swiss roll tin. Spread the jam evenly over the pastry.

Mix together the sugar, ground almonds and rice, then add the eggs. Beat for 4 minutes, until the mixture is smooth and creamy. Spoon onto the jam, spreading it evenly. Sprinkle with the flaked almonds.

Bake in a preheated moderately hot oven, 200°C (400°F), Gas Mark 6, for 20 minutes or until golden. Cool slightly, then cut into slices. Leave in the tin until cold.

Makes 22

VARIATION: Replace the jam with fresh blackcurrants.

Banbury Slices

125 g (4 oz) puff
pastry* or easy
flaky pastry* or
use a 212 g
(7½ oz) packet
puff pastry, thawed
1 small dessert apple,
peeled, cored and
finely diced
125 g (4 oz) currants
1 teaspoon caster
sugar
¼ teaspoon ground
cinnamon
TO FINISH:
50 g (2 oz) icing
sugar, sifted
1½ teaspoons water

Roll out the pastry on a floured
surface to a 30 × 20 cm (12 × 8 inch)
rectangle. Mix together the apple,
currants, sugar and cinnamon and
spread along the centre of the pastry.
Dampen the edges. Fold the long
edges into the centre, overlapping to
enclose the filling. Fold in the ends to
seal and form a neat rectangular shape.

Lift carefully onto a greased
baking sheet, placing the join
underneath. Prick the top well with a
fork and brush lightly with water.
Bake in a preheated hot oven, 220°C
(425°F), Gas Mark 7, for 15 to
20 minutes or until golden brown.
Leave on the baking sheet until cold.

Mix the icing sugar with the water
to make a smooth icing and drizzle
over the top of the pastry. Leave
until set, then cut into slices.
Makes 10 to 12

Minty Yorkshire Slices

Fresh mint is often used to flavour sweet cakes in Yorkshire.
Only a little is used, to give a very subtle flavour.

350 g (12 oz) easy
flaky pastry*
350 g (12 oz)
sultanas
10 mint leaves
50 g (2 oz)
granulated sugar
25 g (1 oz) butter,
melted
25 g (1 oz) caster
sugar

Roll out 200 g (7 oz) of the pastry on
a floured surface and use to line a
20 cm (8 inch) flan tin. Cover with the
sultanas. Chop the mint with a little
of the granulated sugar – this helps to
extract the juices – then mix in the
remaining sugar. Sprinkle over the
sultanas, then pour over the butter.

Roll out the remaining pastry and
place on top; dampen the edges and
seal well. Prick all over with a fork,
brush lightly with water and sprinkle
with the caster sugar.

Bake in a preheated moderately hot
oven, 200°C (400°F), Gas Mark 6, for
20 to 25 minutes or until golden
brown. Cut into slices and serve
warm or cold.
Makes 8

CAKES FOR SLICING

Date and Walnut Cake

150 ml (¼ pint) hot
  water
250 g (8 oz) dates,
  halved and stoned
150 g (5 oz) butter
125 g (4 oz) soft
  brown sugar
2 tablespoons golden
  syrup
2 eggs
275 g (9 oz) self-
  raising flour, sifted
50 g (2 oz) walnuts

Pour the hot water onto the dates
and leave until cold.

Beat the butter and sugar together
until light and fluffy. Beat in the
syrup, then the eggs, one at a time.
Mix in the flour. Roughly chop half
the walnuts, then stir into the mixture
with the dates and soaking water.

Turn the mixture into a lined and
greased 20 cm (8 inch) round cake tin.
Arrange the remaining walnuts on top.

Bake in a preheated moderate oven,
180°C (350°F), Gas Mark 4, for 1 hour
to 1 hour 15 minutes, covering loosely
with foil for the last 30 minutes.
Turn out onto a wire rack to cool.
Makes one 20 cm (8 inch) cake

Walnut Layer Cake

125 g (4 oz)
    margarine
2 tablespoons golden
    syrup
50 g (2 oz) soft
    brown sugar
2 eggs
125 g (4 oz) self-
    raising flour, sifted
50 g (2 oz) walnuts,
    chopped and
    rubbed in a cloth
    to remove skins
1/2 quantity Swiss
    buttercream*

Beat the margarine, syrup and sugar
together until light and fluffy. Add
the eggs one at a time, beating well
between each addition. Fold in the
flour and walnuts; mix until smooth.

Turn the mixture into a lined and
greased 18 cm (7 inch) square cake
tin and bake in a preheated
moderately hot oven, 190°C (375°F),
Gas Mark 5, for 30 minutes or until
firm to touch. Turn out onto a wire
rack to cool.

Split the cake horizontally into
3 slices and sandwich together with
the buttercream. Chill for about
30 minutes before slicing.
Makes one 18 cm (7 inch) cake

Nut and Rum Ring

65 g (2½ oz) caster
  sugar
2 egg yolks
2 eggs
1 tablespoon set
  honey
25 g (1 oz) cornflour
125 g (4 oz) plain
  flour
FRENCH
  BUTTERCREAM:
125 g (4 oz)
  unsalted butter,
  softened
4 tablespoons double
  cream
25 g (1 oz) icing
  sugar, sifted
TO FINISH:
1 quantity sugar
  syrup*, flavoured
  with 2 tablespoons
  rum
200 g (7 oz) apricot
  jam, warmed and
  sieved
50 g (2 oz) each
  hazelnuts and
  walnuts, coarsely
  chopped
1-2 tablespoons icing
  sugar, sifted

Place the sugar, egg yolks and whole eggs in a large heatproof bowl over a pan of hot water and whisk until the whisk leaves a trail. Gently whisk in the honey.

Sift the cornflour and flour together twice. Sift onto the egg mixture and fold in gently, until smooth. Turn into a greased and floured 20 cm (8 inch) ring tin and bake in a preheated moderate oven, 180°C (350°F), Gas Mark 4, for 25 minutes or until springy to touch. Transfer to a wire rack to cool.

Meanwhile, make the buttercream. Beat the butter until light. Whip the cream and sugar together until soft peaks form, then gradually add to the butter, folding in carefully.

Split the cake horizontally into 3 rings. Sprinkle the bottom ring with 3 tablespoons of the sugar syrup, leave until absorbed, then spread with 50 g (2 oz) of the apricot jam.

Place the centre ring neatly on top and sprinkle with 4 tablespoons of the sugar syrup. Leave until absorbed, then spread the buttercream evenly over the surface. Place the remaining ring on top and sprinkle with the remaining syrup. Chill for 1 hour.

Place the cake on a wire rack over a bowl. Bring the remaining apricot jam to the boil and carefully pour over the cake to coat the entire surface; allow the surplus jam to drain into the bowl. Sprinkle the nuts evenly over the entire surface, then dust with icing sugar.

Makes one 20 cm (8 inch) cake
NOTE: Do use *un*salted butter for the buttercream – it gives a far better result than salted.

For extra flavour, add rum to taste to the apricot jam.

Almond Cake

75 g (3 oz) butter
50 g (2 oz) vegetable fat
150 g (5 oz) caster sugar
2 drops of almond essence
50 g (2 oz) ground almonds
finely grated rind of ½ lemon
2 large eggs, beaten
125 g (4 oz) plain flour, sifted
15 g (½ oz) flaked almonds
2 teaspoons icing sugar, sifted

Beat the butter, fat, caster sugar and almond essence together until light and fluffy. Beat in the ground almonds and lemon rind. Add the eggs a little at a time, beating well between each addition, then fold in the flour. Turn into a greased and floured 15 cm (6 inch) round cake tin, smooth the top and sprinkle on the flaked almonds and icing sugar.

Bake in a preheated moderate oven, 180°C (350°F), Gas Mark 4, for 45 to 50 minutes or until firm to touch. Leave in the tin for 5 minutes, then turn out and cool on a wire rack.

Makes one 15 cm (6 inch) cake

Cherry and Coconut Cake

150 g (5 oz)
  self-raising flour
¼ teaspoon salt
125 g (4 oz) caster
  sugar
75 g (3 oz) butter
1 egg
5 tablespoons milk
175 g (6 oz) glacé
  cherries, washed,
  drained and halved
50 g (2 oz)
  desiccated coconut
1 tablespoon
  demerara sugar

Sift the flour and salt into a bowl, stir in the caster sugar, then rub in the butter until the mixture resembles breadcrumbs.

Beat the egg and milk together. Mix the cherries and the coconut together. Add both to the flour mixture and fold in gently.

Turn the mixture into a greased and floured 500 g (1 lb) loaf tin and sprinkle with the demerara sugar. Bake in a preheated moderate oven, 180°C (350°F), Gas Mark 4, for 45 to 50 minutes or until firm to touch. Transfer to a wire rack to cool.
Makes one 500 g (1 lb) loaf

Coconut Cake

2 eggs
6 tablespoons milk
   (approximately)
125 g (4 oz) caster
   sugar
75 g (3 oz)
   desiccated coconut
175 g (6 oz) plain
   flour
2 teaspoons baking
   powder
125 g (4 oz) butter
TOPPING:
2 tablespoons
   desiccated coconut
1 tablespoon sugar

Break the eggs into a measuring jug, beat lightly, then add milk to make up to 150 ml (¼ pint). Mix in half the sugar and the coconut. Leave to stand for 30 minutes.

Sift the flour and baking powder into a bowl, then stir in the remaining sugar. Rub in the butter until the mixture resembles breadcrumbs, then add the coconut mixture. Mix gently but thoroughly together.

Turn the mixture into a greased and floured 500 g (1 lb) loaf tin. Mix together the coconut and sugar for the topping and sprinkle over the top. Bake in a preheated moderately hot oven, 190°C (375°F), Gas Mark 5, for 45 to 50 minutes or until firm to touch. Cool on a wire rack. Serve with butter and jam.
Makes one 500 g (1 lb) loaf

Ginger Sponge Cake

125 g (4 oz)
   self-raising flour
2 teaspoons ground
   ginger
1/2 teaspoon baking
   powder
1/4 teaspoon salt
75 g (3 oz)
   margarine
6 tablespoons golden
   syrup
50 g (2 oz) soft
   brown sugar
2 eggs, beaten
15 g (1/2 oz) flaked
   almonds

Sift the flour, ginger, baking powder and salt together in a large bowl and rub in the margarine until the mixture resembles breadcrumbs. Add the syrup, sugar and eggs and beat well using a wooden spoon for about 2 minutes, until the mixture is smooth and creamy.

Turn the mixture into a greased and lined 18 cm (7 inch) square cake tin and sprinkle the almonds evenly over the top. Bake in a preheated moderate oven, 180°C (350°F), Gas Mark 4, for 30 minutes or until firm to touch. Turn out and cool on a wire rack.

Makes 15 slices

Dutch Honey Cake

125 g (4 oz)
   self-raising flour
1 teaspoon ground
   ginger
1/2 teaspoon baking
   powder
1/4 teaspoon salt
75 g (3 oz)
   margarine
6 tablespoons clear
   honey
50 g (2 oz) soft
   brown sugar
1 egg, beaten
2 tablespoons milk
15 g (1/2 oz) flaked
   almonds

Sift the flour, ginger, baking powder and salt together into a bowl and rub in the margarine until the mixture resembles breadcrumbs. Add the honey, sugar, egg and milk and beat thoroughly for about 2 minutes, until the mixture is smooth and creamy.

Turn the mixture into a greased and lined 18 cm (7 inch) square cake tin and sprinkle the almonds evenly over the top. Bake in a preheated moderate oven, 180°C (350°F), Gas Mark 4, for 30 minutes, or until firm to touch. Turn out and cool on a wire rack.

Serve lightly spread with unsalted butter, if liked.

Makes 15 slices

Lemon Ginger Cake

250 g (8 oz) golden syrup
125 g (4 oz) butter
250 g (8 oz) lemon marmalade
1 egg, beaten
250 g (8 oz) plain flour
2 teaspoons baking powder
1 teaspoon ground ginger

Heat the syrup and butter until melted, remove from the heat and stir in the marmalade and egg. Leave until cold.

Sift the flour, baking powder and ginger together in a large bowl. Add the syrup mixture and beat until thoroughly blended.

Turn the mixture into a lined and greased 20 cm (8 inch) square cake tin and bake in a preheated moderate oven, 180°C (350°F), Gas Mark 4, for 45 minutes or until firm to touch. Turn out and cool on a wire rack.

Makes 15 to 20 slices

Rich Dark Chocolate Cake

175 g (6 oz)
  self-raising flour
50 g (2 oz) cocoa
  powder
1/4 teaspoon baking
  powder
175 g (6 oz) caster
  sugar
25 g (1 oz)
  desiccated coconut
125 g (4 oz) margarine
2 eggs
6 tablespoons golden
  syrup
150 ml (1/4 pint) milk
CHOCOLATE ICING:
4 tablespoons milk
50 g (2 oz) butter
25 g (1 oz) caster
  sugar
50 g (2 oz) plain
  chocolate, grated
250 g (8 oz) icing
  sugar, sifted
GLACÉ ICING:
75 g (3 oz) icing
  sugar, sifted
3 teaspoons water

Sift the flour, cocoa and baking powder into a bowl. Stir in the sugar and coconut, then rub in the margarine. Beat the eggs, syrup and milk together, add to the flour mixture and beat well until smooth.

Turn the mixture into a greased and floured 23 cm (9 inch) sandwich tin and bake in a preheated cool oven, 150°C (300°F), Gas Mark 2, for 1 hour or until firm to touch. Invert onto a wire rack to cool.

To make the chocolate icing, heat the milk, butter, caster sugar and chocolate gently in a saucepan until melted. Pour onto the icing sugar in a bowl and beat well until smooth.

Pour onto the flat base of the cake and spread with a palette knife to cover the cake completely. Immediately mix the icing sugar and water for the glacé icing until smooth and, using a No. 3 writing nozzle, pipe lines across the top of the chocolate icing. With a cocktail stick draw lines in alternate directions across the lines of icing to create a feathered design.
Makes one 23 cm (9 inch) cake

Chocolate and Banana Cake

125 g (4 oz) butter
125 g (4 oz) caster
  sugar
25 g (1 oz) honey
2 eggs
1 banana, mashed
150 g (5 oz)
  self-raising flour
3 tablespoons cocoa
  powder
FILLING:
1/4 quantity Swiss
  buttercream*
TO DECORATE:
1 quantity Ganache*

Cream the butter and sugar together until light and fluffy. Beat in the honey, then the eggs, one at a time. Beat in the banana. Sift the flour and cocoa together onto the mixture and fold in.

Divide between two greased and floured 18 cm (7 inch) sandwich tins and bake in a preheated moderate oven, 180°C (350°F), Gas Mark 4, for 30 to 35 minutes. Cool on a wire rack.

Sandwich the cakes together with the buttercream. Chill for 30 minutes, then cover with the ganache.
Makes one 18 cm (7 inch) cake

Almond Cherry Cake

75 g (3 oz) ground
    almonds
225 g (7½ oz) caster
    sugar
3 eggs, beaten
150 g (5 oz) butter,
    softened
150 g (5 oz) plain
    flour, sifted
250 g (8 oz) glacé
    cherries, halved,
    washed and
    drained
25 g (1 oz)
    desiccated coconut

Mix the ground almonds and 75 g (3 oz) of the sugar together in a bowl. Mix to a paste with 2 tablespoons of the egg. Set aside.

Beat the butter and remaining sugar together until light and fluffy. Beat in the remaining egg a little at a time, adding 2 tablespoons of the flour when half the egg is used. Fold in the remaining flour.

Mix the cherries and coconut together and add to the mixture, stirring gently to distribute evenly.

Turn half the mixture into a lined 18 cm (7 inch) cake tin. Roll out the almond paste to fit just inside the tin and place on top of the mixture, pressing down gently. Place the remaining cake mixture on top and smooth the surface. Bake in a pre-heated moderate oven, 160°C (325°F), Gas Mark 3, for 1¼ hours; cover with foil for the last 30 minutes to prevent over-browning. Leave in the tin for 5 minutes, then turn onto a wire rack to cool.

Makes one 18 cm (7 inch) cake

Carrot and Fruit Cake

125 g (4 oz) soft
  brown sugar
6 tablespoons clear
  honey
175 g (6 oz) carrot,
  finely grated
125 g (4 oz) seedless
  raisins
50 g (2 oz) dates,
  chopped
¾ teaspoon ground
  nutmeg
125 g (4 oz) butter
150 ml (¼ pint)
  water
1 egg, beaten
125 g (4 oz)
  wholemeal flour
125 g (4 oz) plain
  flour, sifted
2 teaspoons baking
  powder

Mix the sugar, honey, carrot, raisins, dates, nutmeg, butter and water together in a saucepan. Bring to the boil and simmer for 5 minutes. Turn into a mixing bowl and leave until cold.

Stir in the egg. Mix the flours and baking powder together and sprinkle over the mixture. Mix together thoroughly.

Turn the mixture into a greased and floured 23 cm (9 inch) cake tin and bake in a preheated moderate oven, 180°C (350°F), Gas Mark 4, for 55 to 60 minutes or until firm to touch. Cool on a wire rack.

Makes one 23 cm (9 inch) cake

Dundee Cake

175 g (6 oz) margarine
150 g (5 oz) soft brown sugar
1 teaspoon black treacle
finely grated rind of 1 orange and ½ lemon
25 g (1 oz) ground almonds
4 eggs, beaten
250 g (8 oz) plain flour, sifted
½ teaspoon baking powder
350 g (12 oz) sultanas
1 tablespoon whisky
50 g (2 oz) split blanched almonds

Beat the margarine, sugar, treacle, orange and lemon rinds and ground almonds together until light. Add the eggs a little at a time, beating well between each addition.

Fold in the flour and baking powder, then add the sultanas and whisky, mixing in well, but gently.

Turn the mixture into a lined and greased 18 cm (7 inch) cake tin; smooth the surface and arrange the almonds on top.

Bake in a preheated cool oven, 140°C (275°F), Gas Mark 1, for 1¾ to 2 hours, until a skewer inserted into the centre comes out clean; cover with foil for the last 30 minutes to prevent over-browning. Leave in the tin for 5 minutes, then turn onto a wire rack to cool.

Makes one 18 cm (7 inch) cake

Wholemeal Farmhouse Cake

This is an excellent way of using up leftover cake; if fruit cake is used, decrease the amount of fruit in the recipe. Any kind of dried fruit can be used – try adding chopped dates.

125 g (4 oz) wholemeal flour
2 teaspoons baking powder
125 g (4 oz) cake crumbs
125 g (4 oz) demerara sugar
50 g (2 oz) margarine
2 eggs
120 ml (4 fl oz) milk (approximately)
175 g (6 oz) dried mixed fruit
2 teaspoons demerara sugar to finish

Mix the flour, baking powder, cake crumbs and sugar together and rub in the margarine. Break the eggs into a measuring jug, beat lightly, and make up to 175 ml (6 fl oz) with milk. Add to the flour mixture with the fruit and beat until thoroughly mixed.

Turn the mixture into a greased and floured 500 g (1 lb) loaf tin and sprinkle with the demerara sugar. Bake in a preheated moderately hot oven, 200°C (400°F), Gas Mark 6, for 40 to 50 minutes, until golden and firm to touch. Turn out and cool on a wire rack.

Makes one 500 g (1 lb) loaf

Madeira Cake

175 g (6 oz) butter,
  softened
175 g (6 oz) caster
  sugar
15 g (½ oz) ground
  almonds
3 drops vanilla
  essence
3 eggs, beaten
175 g (6 oz)
  self-raising flour,
  sifted
1 slice citron peel

Cream the butter and sugar together until light and fluffy. Stir in the almonds and vanilla essence. Add the eggs a little at a time, beating well between each addition. Gently mix in the flour.

Turn the mixture into a lined and greased 18 cm (7 inch) cake tin and flatten slightly. Bake in a preheated moderate oven, 160°C (325°F), Gas Mark 3, for 45 minutes. Place the citron peel on top of the cake and bake for a further 20 minutes or until firm to touch. Cool on a wire rack.

Makes one 18 cm (7 inch) cake

VARIATION: Warm 1 tablespoon caraway seeds and add with the flour. Replace the citron peel with a few caraway seeds sprinkled over the top of the cake.

Battenberg

125 g (4 oz)
   margarine
125 g (4 oz) caster
   sugar
few drops of almond
   essence (optional)
2 large eggs, beaten
50 g (2 oz)
   self-raising flour,
   sifted
50 g (2 oz) plain
   flour, sifted
few drops of pink
   food colouring
3 tablespoons apricot
   jam, warmed and
   sieved
250 g (8 oz)
   marzipan

Beat the margarine and sugar together with the almond essence, if using, until light and fluffy. Add the eggs a little at a time, beating between each addition. Fold in the flours.

Divide the mixture in half and colour one half pink. Turn the pink mixture into a lined and greased 1 kg (2 lb) loaf tin. Cover with a piece of greased greaseproof paper. Spread the plain mixture on top.

Bake in a preheated moderate oven, 180°C (350°F), Gas Mark 4, for 30 to 35 minutes or until firm to touch.

Turn out onto a wire rack, remove the paper and leave to cool.

Trim the two halves carefully to remove all crust, then cut each piece in half lengthways. Sandwich the strips together with jam, alternating colours.

Roll out the marzipan to the same length as the cake and 4 times as wide; spread with jam. Place the cake on the long side of the marzipan and turn it 4 times to enclose the cake completely. Neaten the join and edges.

Makes one battenberg

Simnel Cake

150 g (5 oz) butter
150 g (5 oz) soft
  brown sugar
2 eggs, beaten
150 g (5 oz) plain
  flour
1/2 teaspoon baking
  powder
1 teaspoon ground
  mixed spice
125 g (4 oz)
  sultanas
175 g (6 oz) currants
50 g (2 oz) cut
  mixed peel
juice of 1 orange
ALMOND PASTE:
250 g (8 oz) ground
  almonds
250 g (8 oz) caster
  sugar
1 egg, beaten
2 drops almond
  essence
TO FINISH:
50 g (2 oz) apricot
  jam, warmed and
  sieved
little beaten egg
125 g (4 oz) icing
  sugar, sifted
1 tablespoon water
few drops of yellow
  food colouring

First make the almond paste: mix the ground almonds and sugar together in a bowl. Add the egg and almond essence and mix to form a stiff paste; set aside.

For the cake, beat the butter and sugar together until light and fluffy, then gradually add the eggs, beating well between each addition.

Sift the flour, baking powder and spice together and fold into the creamed mixture. Add the dried fruit, peel and orange juice and mix until evenly distributed.

Weigh 500 g (1 lb) of the mixture and place in a lined and greased 18 cm (7 inch) round cake tin. Smooth the surface.

Roll out half the almond paste to fit just inside the tin and place on top of the cake mixture. Place the remaining cake mixture on top and smooth the surface.

Bake in a preheated moderate oven, 180°C (350°F), Gas Mark 4, for 1 hour 20 minutes or until a skewer inserted into the cake comes out clean. Leave in the tin to cool.

Brush the top of the cake with the jam. Shape the remaining almond paste into a rope and fit it round the edge of the cake. Press it flat with a fork, making a serrated wall, and brush lightly with beaten egg. Place in a preheated very hot oven, 240°C (475°F), Gas Mark 9, for a few minutes to brown slightly.

Mix the icing sugar with the water and food colouring to make a smooth icing. Pour onto the centre of the cake and spread evenly. Decorate as liked, with sweet eggs or chicks.

Make one 18 cm (7 inch) cake
NOTE: Bought marzipan is too firm to be suitable for this recipe.

Orange Cake

175 g (6 oz) butter
175 g (6 oz) caster
  sugar
3 eggs, beaten
finely grated rind and
  juice of 1 orange
175 g (6 oz) self-
  raising flour, sifted
TO FINISH:
142 ml (¼ pint)
  double cream,
  whipped
125 g (4 oz) icing
  sugar, sifted
1 tablespoon orange
  juice
orange rind shreds

Beat the butter and sugar together until light and fluffy. Add the eggs a little at a time, beating well between each addition. Stir in the orange rind. Add the flour and orange juice and mix gently until thoroughly blended.

Turn the mixture into 2 greased and floured 18 cm (7 inch) sandwich tins and bake in a preheated moderate oven; 180°C (350°F), Gas Mark 4, for 30 minutes. Cool on a wire rack.

Sandwich the cakes together with the cream. Beat the icing sugar and orange juice together until smooth. Spread on top of the cake and decorate with orange shreds.

Makes one 18 cm (7 inch) cake

Swiss Roll

3 eggs
75 g (3 oz) caster
    sugar
75 g (3 oz) plain
    flour, sifted
TO FINISH:
caster sugar for
    sprinkling
6 tablespoons
    raspberry jam
    (approximately)

Whisk the eggs and sugar together in a large bowl until the whisk leaves a trail, then fold in the flour. Turn the mixture into a lined and greased 20 × 30 cm (8 × 12 inch) Swiss roll tin and smooth the surface.

Bake in a preheated moderately hot oven, 200°C (400°F), Gas Mark 6, for 10 to 12 minutes or until pale golden and springy to touch.

Sprinkle a sheet of greaseproof paper liberally with sugar and place on a slightly damp, clean cloth. Turn the sponge out onto the sugared paper and remove the lining paper. Spread the sponge with jam and carefully roll up from the short edge, using the cloth to help you. Trim the edges. Transfer to a wire rack to cool.

Makes one Swiss roll

Chocolate Swiss Roll

40 g (1½ oz)
    self-raising flour
15 g (½ oz) cocoa
    powder
3 eggs
50 g (2 oz) caster
    sugar
½ quantity Swiss
    buttercream*

Sift flour and cocoa together twice. Whisk the eggs and sugar together in a large bowl until the whisk leaves a trail. Fold in the flour mixture.

Turn the mixture into a lined, greased and floured 20 × 30 cm (8 × 12 inch) Swiss roll tin and smooth the surface. Bake in a preheated moderately hot oven, 200°C (400°F), Gas Mark 6, for 12 to 14 minutes or until springy to touch.

Turn out onto lightly sugared greaseproof paper placed on a slightly damp, clean cloth and remove the lining paper. Roll up tightly from the short edge with the sugared paper inside. Leave to cool for about 20 minutes.

Unroll the sponge, remove the paper and spread with the buttercream. Re-roll and trim the edges. Chill until required.

Makes one Swiss roll

SPECIAL OCCASION GÂTEAUX

Apricot and Almond Meringue

- 4 egg whites
- 250 g (8 oz) caster sugar
- 50 g (2 oz) dried apricots, diced
- 50 g (2 oz) whole blanched almonds, quartered
- 284 ml (½ pint) double or whipping cream, whipped
- few flaked almonds, toasted, to decorate

Draw two 20 cm (8 inch) rounds on silicone paper placed on baking sheets.

Whisk the egg whites until soft peaks form, then gradually whisk in the sugar until the mixture is firm. Fold in the apricots and almonds.

Spoon the mixture over the two rounds. Bake in a preheated cool oven, 140°C (275°F), Gas Mark 1, for 50 minutes. Cool on a wire rack.

Reserve a little of the cream and sandwich the meringue rounds together with the remainder, 2 hours before serving.

Using the reserved cream, pipe rosettes around the edge of the meringue and top with the almonds.

Serves 6 to 8

Paris Brest

125 g (4 oz) choux
  pastry*
150 ml (¼ pint)
  crème pâtissière*
few drops of coffee
  essence (optional)
284 ml (½ pint)
  whipping cream
ICING:
125 g (4 oz) icing
  sugar, sifted
1 tablespoon water
few drops of coffee
  essence

Spoon the choux pastry into a piping bag fitted with a 1 cm (½ inch) plain nozzle and pipe a double 20 cm (8 inch) ring on a dampened baking sheet.

Bake in a preheated hot oven, 220°C (425°F), Gas Mark 7, for 20 minutes. Lower the heat to 180°C (350°F), Gas Mark 4, and bake for a further 10 to 15 minutes, until golden brown, hollow and well dried out. Split the cake horizontally and cool on a wire rack.

Flavour the crème pâtissière with coffee essence, to taste, if using. Whip the cream and fold into the crème pâtissière and use to sandwich the layers together.

Mix the icing sugar and water, adding coffee essence to taste. Spoon over the cake and leave to set.

Serves 8

Hazelnut Roulade

3 eggs
65 g (2½ oz) caster sugar
15 g (½ oz) plain flour
50 g (2 oz) ground hazelnuts
142 ml (¼ pint) double cream, whipped
TO FINISH:
caster sugar for sprinkling
sifted icing sugar, to decorate

Whisk the eggs and sugar together until the whisk leaves a trail. Sift the flour onto the mixture, add the nuts and carefully fold together. Turn into a lined and greased 20 × 30 cm (8 × 12 inch) Swiss roll tin. Bake in a preheated moderately hot oven, 200°C (400°F), Gas Mark 6, for 10 to 12 minutes or until springy to touch.

Turn out onto lightly sugared, greaseproof paper placed on a damp, clean tea-towel. Remove the lining paper and trim the edges if necessary. Carefully roll up the sponge from the short edge with the sugared paper inside and leave until cold. Unroll the sponge and remove paper. Spread with the cream, then roll up again. Chill until required and sprinkle liberally with icing sugar to serve.
Serves 8

Tia Maria Torten

CAKE MIXTURE:

75 g (3 oz)
    self-raising flour
3 tablespoons cocoa
    powder
4 eggs
75 g (3 oz) caster
    sugar

TO FINISH:

1 quantity Tia
    Maria-flavoured
    sugar syrup*
1 quantity Swiss
    buttercream*
few drops coffee
    essence
25 g (1 oz) chocolate
    sugar strands
12 small Florentine
    biscuits (page 58)

First make up the cake mixture as for Chocolate Swiss Roll (page 46). Divide between two greased and floured 23 cm (9 inch) cake tins and bake in a preheated moderately hot oven, 200°C (400°F), Gas Mark 6, for 15 to 20 minutes or until springy to touch. Cool on a wire rack.

Place one sponge on a cake board and drizzle over less than half the syrup. Leave for about 10 minutes until absorbed. Flavour the butter cream with coffee essence to taste. Spread one-third over the soaked sponge. Place the other sponge on top and drizzle over the remaining syrup; leave for 10 minutes.

Reserve 3 tablespoons of the remaining buttercream; use the rest to coat the top and side of the cake. Coat the side with chocolate sugar strands. Lightly mark the top with a fork, then mark into 12 sections. Pipe a buttercream rosette on each portion and top with a florentine.
Serves 12

Rum and Blackcurrant Torten

CAKE MIXTURE:
75 g (3 oz)
self-raising flour
3 tablespoons cocoa
powder
4 eggs
75 g (3 oz) caster
sugar

TO FINISH:
1 quantity
rum-flavoured
sugar syrup*
4 tablespoons
blackcurrant
conserve
284 ml (½ pint)
double cream,
whipped
50 g (2 oz) flaked
almonds, toasted
2-3 teaspoons cocoa
powder, sifted, for
sprinkling

First make two 23 cm (9 inch) cakes as for Tipsy Mandarin Torten (opposite). Cool on a wire rack.

Place one sponge on a cake board and drizzle over slightly less than half the syrup. Leave for about 10 minutes until absorbed, then spread with 3 tablespoons of the conserve and one third of the cream. Place the other sponge on top and drizzle over the remaining syrup; leave for 10 minutes.

Reserve 3 tablespoons of the remaining cream for decoration; use the rest to coat the top and side of the cake. Press the almonds onto the side of the cake. Chill for 30 minutes.

Lightly mark the top into 12 sections. Using a piping bag fitted with a star nozzle, pipe an open rosette of cream on each portion and fill with the remaining conserve. Dust the centre of the cake with cocoa powder.

Serves 12

52

Tipsy Mandarin Torten

CAKE MIXTURE:
75 g (3 oz)
   self-raising flour
3 tablespoons cocoa
   powder
4 eggs
75 g (3 oz) caster
   sugar

TO FINISH:
1 quantity Grand
   Marnier-flavoured
   sugar syrup*
1 tablespoon
   tangerine or mild
   orange marmalade
284 ml (½ pint)
   double cream,
   whipped
16-18 Langue de
   chat biscuits,
   halved (page 12)
1 × 312 g (11 oz)
   can mandarin
   segments, drained
50 g (2 oz) plain
   chocolate, grated

First make up the cake mixture as for Chocolate Swiss Roll (page 46). Divide between two greased and floured 23 cm (9 inch) cake tins and bake in a preheated moderately hot oven, 200°C (400°F), Gas Mark 6, for 15 to 20 minutes or until springy to touch. Cool on a wire rack.

Place one sponge on a serving plate and drizzle over slightly less than half the syrup. Leave for 10 minutes until the syrup is absorbed, then spread with the marmalade and about one third of the cream. Place the other sponge on top and drizzle over the remaining syrup. Leave for 10 minutes. Cover the top and side of the cake with the remaining cream and chill for 30 minutes.

Lightly mark the top into 12 sections. Press the halved biscuits around the side of the cake, rounded side uppermost. Arrange the mandarins around the top edge and sprinkle chocolate in the centre.
Serves 12

Almond and Hazelnut Gâteau

This is a simplified version of a world-famous dessert served at La Pyramide restaurant in Vienne, France. It is certainly worthy of its reputation – even this simple version is delicious.

50 g (2 oz) ground almonds
40 g (1½ oz) hazelnuts, finely chopped
75 g (3 oz) caster sugar
3 egg whites
CHOCOLATE CREAM:
125 g (4 oz) plain chocolate, broken into pieces
25 g (1 oz) unsalted butter
120 ml (4 fl oz) double cream
ORANGE CREAM:
125 g (4 oz) unsalted butter, softened
142 ml (5 fl oz) double cream
25 g (1 oz) caster sugar
finely grated rind of ½ orange
TO FINISH:
50 g (2 oz) hazelnuts, finely chopped and toasted
icing sugar, sifted, for sprinkling

Mix together the ground almonds, hazelnuts and half the sugar.

Whisk the egg whites until soft peaks form; then whisk in the remaining sugar until stiff. Carefully fold in the nut mixture and spread evenly into a lined and greased 20 × 30 cm (8 × 12 inch) Swiss roll tin.

Bake in a preheated moderately hot oven, 200°C (400°F), Gas Mark 6, for about 20 minutes, until the sponge is a light coffee colour. Leave to cool in the tin while making the chocolate cream.

Place the chocolate in a heatproof bowl over a pan of hot water until melted. Add the butter and stir until melted. Remove from heat and set aside to cool slightly. Whip the cream until thick but not too stiff, then fold into the lukewarm chocolate until smooth and shiny. Set aside while making the orange cream.

Beat the butter until soft and light. Whip the cream with the sugar until thick but not too stiff, then add to the butter a little at a time, mixing gently. Stir in the orange rind.

Trim the edges of the sponge and cut into 3 equal pieces 20 cm (8 inches) long. Place one piece on a cake board and spread with the chocolate cream. Top with another slice and chill until set. Spread with half the orange cream and top with the remaining nut slice.

Cover completely with remaining orange cream and coat the top and sides with the hazelnuts. Sprinkle the top with icing sugar. Serve chilled.
Serves 10

FOREIGN CAKES

Sacher Torte

125 g (4 oz) butter
125 g (4 oz) caster sugar
25 g (1 oz) ground almonds
4 eggs, separated
175 g (6 oz) plain chocolate, melted
125 g (4 oz) self-raising flour
2 tablespoons raspberry conserve
1 quantity Ganache*

Beat the butter, sugar and ground almonds together until light and fluffy. Beat in the egg yolks one at a time. Gradually beat in the cooled chocolate.

Sift the flour onto the mixture and fold in gently. Whisk the egg whites until soft peaks form, then carefully fold into the mixture.

Turn into a greased and floured 20 cm (8 in) cake tin and smooth the surface. Bake in a preheated moderate oven, 180°C (350°F), Gas Mark 4, for 55 minutes or until firm to touch. Leave in the tin for 5 minutes, then cool on a wire rack.

Split the cake in half and sandwich together with the conserve, then cover with the melted ganache.
Makes one 20 cm (8 inch) cake

Ganache Slices

200 g (7 oz)
  self-raising flour
50 g (2 oz) cocoa
1/4 teaspoon baking
  powder
175 g (6 oz) caster
  sugar
125 g (4 oz)
  margarine
2 eggs, beaten
6 tablespoons golden
  syrup
150 ml (1/4 pint) milk
1/2 quantity Swiss
  buttercream*
1 quantity Ganache*
250 g (8 oz)
  marzipan
50 g (2 oz) plain
  chocolate, melted
2 tablespoons
  chocolate sugar
  strands

Sift the flour, cocoa and baking powder into a bowl, stir in the sugar, then rub in the margarine. Mix the eggs, syrup and milk together, add to the flour mixture and whisk until smooth.

Turn the mixture into a greased and floured 1 kg (2 lb) loaf tin and bake in a preheated moderate oven, 160°C (325°F), Gas Mark 3, for 50 to 60 minutes or until firm to touch. Cool on a wire rack. Trim to an oblong, then cut into 3 layers.

Mix the buttercream with half the ganache. Sandwich the layers together with most of this mixture and spread the remainder all over the cake. Chill the remaining ganache.

Roll out the marzipan quite thinly and use to cover the cake completely, pressing it smoothly onto the surface; trim off any excess. Chill.

Put the melted chocolate in a grease-proof paper piping bag and drizzle chocolate across the top of the cake.

Form the remaining chilled ganache into 8 small balls and roll in the chocolate sugar strands. Place at 2.5 cm (1 inch) intervals along the centre of the cake. Serve sliced.

Makes 10

Florentines

75 g (3 oz) flaked almonds
50 g (2 oz) cut mixed peel
50 g (2 oz) glacé cherries, quartered
50 g (2 oz) butter, melted
50 g (2 oz) caster sugar
1 tablespoon double cream
125 g (4 oz) plain chocolate, melted

Mix the almonds, peel and cherries together. Stir into the butter, together with the sugar and cream. Leave until cold. Place teaspoonfuls of the mixture well apart on greased and floured baking sheets.

Bake in a preheated moderately hot oven, 190°C (375°F), Gas Mark 5, for about 6 to 8 minutes until pale golden brown round the edge. Reshape, using a large pastry cutter, and leave on the baking sheet until almost cold. Transfer to a wire rack, flat sides up, and spread thinly with the melted chocolate.

Makes about 30

Cheese Blintzes

75 g (3 oz) plain flour
1 egg, beaten
1 tablespoon butter, melted
175 ml (6 fl oz) milk
227 g (8 oz) cream cheese
1 tablespoon caster sugar
3 tablespoons icing sugar, sifted
¼ teaspoon ground cinnamon
25 g (1 oz) butter for frying

Sift the flour into a bowl, add the egg and beat well together. Beat in the melted butter and milk gradually to make a thin batter and leave for 1 hour.

Heat a 15 cm (6 inch) omelet pan and add a few drops of oil. Pour in enough batter to coat the bottom evenly. Cook until the underside is starting to brown and the top surface is dry; *do not turn* and cook the other side. Place on a work surface cooked side up. Repeat with the remaining batter, making 12 pancakes in all.

Mix the cream cheese and caster sugar together and divide equally between the pancakes. Fold them round the filling to make neat rectangular parcels about 7.5 × 3.5 cm (3 × 1½ inches). Mix the icing sugar and cinnamon together and roll the parcels in it.

Melt the butter in a frying pan, add the blintzes and fry gently until golden. Serve immediately, with pouring cream and blackcurrant or black cherry conserve.

Makes 10 to 12

Banana Roulade

40 g (1½ oz)
  self-raising flour
15 g (½ oz) cocoa
  powder
3 eggs
50 g (2 oz) caster
  sugar
FILLING:
3 tablespoons sugar
  syrup,* flavoured
  with anissette
  liqueur or rum
½ quantity Swiss
  buttercream*
1 banana
TO FINISH:
little lemon juice
icing sugar, sifted,
  for sprinkling

Sift the flour and cocoa together twice. Whisk the eggs and sugar together until the whisk leaves a trail. Fold in the flour and cocoa thoroughly.

Turn into a lined and greased 18 × 28 cm (7 × 11 inch) Swiss roll tin and smooth the surface. Bake in a preheated moderately hot oven, 200°C (400°F), Gas Mark 6, for 12 to 14 minutes or until springy to touch.

Turn out onto lightly sugared paper on a damp cloth and remove the lining paper. Using the cloth to help, roll up the sponge from the short edge with the sugared paper inside and leave to cool.

Unroll sponge, remove paper and sprinkle with the syrup. Cover with the buttercream, then lay the banana across the roll, a little in from the edge. Roll up the sponge with the banana inside. Trim ends and brush the ends of the banana with lemon juice. Dust with icing sugar. Chill for 1 hour.
Makes one roulade

Strawberry Shortcakes

250 g (8 oz) plain
    flour
3 teaspoons baking
    powder
1/2 teaspoon salt
65 g (2½ oz) butter
25 g (1 oz) caster
    sugar
150 ml (¼ pint)
    sour milk (see
    note)
2 egg yolks
FILLING:
142 ml (¼ pint)
    double cream,
    whipped
500 g (1 lb)
    strawberries,
    halved
50 g (2 oz) caster
    sugar

Sift the flour, baking powder and salt into a bowl and rub in the butter until the mixture resembles breadcrumbs. Make a well in the centre and add the sugar, milk and egg yolks. Mix them together in the well, then gradually stir in the dry ingredients and mix to a soft dough.

Divide the dough into 6 equal portions, shape into balls and place on a greased baking sheet. Flatten a little and bake in a preheated moderately hot oven, 190°C (375°F), Gas Mark 5, for 20 minutes, until golden.

Split open while still warm and spread with two thirds of the cream. Mix together the strawberries and sugar and put a spoonful on one half of each shortcake. Place the other half on top. Top each with a swirl of cream and a few strawberry halves.

Makes 6

NOTE: Sour milk is made by adding a squeeze of lemon juice to fresh milk.

French Pear Tart

250 g (8 oz) crispy
   butter pastry*
450 ml (¾ pint)
   crème pâtissière*
2 firm pears, peeled
   and cored
50 g (2 oz) sugar

Roll out the pastry on a floured surface and use to line a 23 cm (9 inch) flan ring placed on a baking sheet. Bake 'blind' in a preheated moderately hot oven, 200°C (400°F), Gas Mark 6, for 20 minutes, removing the paper and beans after 15 minutes.

Spread the crème pâtissière evenly in the flan case. Cut the pears in half lengthways, then into thin slices. Place neatly in circles on the custard, overlapping slightly. Sprinkle the sugar evenly over the surface and place under a preheated very hot grill until the sugar melts and caramelizes.

Makes one 23 cm (9 inch) tart

NOTE: The grill must be very hot indeed or the operation will take too long and the custard will separate. As an alternative, omit the sugar, place the tart in a preheated moderate oven, 180°C (350°F), Gas Mark 4, for 5 minutes, then brush the pears with 2 tablespoons boiled and sieved apricot jam.

Tart Amandine

250 g (8 oz) short
  flan pastry*
125 g (4 oz) butter
125 g (4 oz) caster
  sugar
3 eggs
125 g (4 oz) ground
  almonds
3 tablespoons
  raspberry conserve
50 g (2 oz) icing
  sugar, sifted
1-2 teaspoons water
25 g (1 oz) flaked
  almonds

Roll out the pastry on a floured surface and use to line a 23 cm (9 inch) flan ring placed on a baking sheet. Bake 'blind' in a preheated moderately hot oven, 200°C (400°F), Gas Mark 6, for 20 minutes; remove the paper and beans after 15 minutes.

Beat the butter and caster sugar together until light and fluffy. Add the eggs one at a time, beating well after each addition. Mix in the ground almonds.

Spread the conserve over the base of the flan case and cover with the almond mixture. Bake in a preheated moderate oven, 180°C (350°F), Gas Mark 4, for 30 to 35 minutes or until firm to touch.

Mix the icing sugar with enough water to make a thin pouring consistency and spread over the tart while still hot. Sprinkle with the almonds and return to the oven for 5 minutes. Serve warm or cold.

Makes one 23 cm (9 inch) tart

Linzer Torten

LINZER PASTRY:
125 g (4 oz) butter
*175 g (6 oz) icing
sugar, sifted*
1 egg, beaten
*finely grated rind of
1 lemon*
*125 g (4 oz) ground
almonds or
hazelnuts*
*125 g (4 oz) plain
flour, sifted*
FILLING:
*2 tablespoons
raspberry conserve*
TO FINISH:
*2 tablespoons apricot
jam, boiled and
sieved*

Cream the butter and icing sugar together until light and fluffy, then beat in the egg and lemon rind. Mix the ground nuts and flour together and fold into the butter mixture to make a smooth, pliable dough. Turn out onto a floured surface and shape into a flattened ball; wrap in cling film and chill for 1 hour.

Lightly butter a loose-bottomed 23 cm (9 inch) flan tin. Carefully roll out the dough on a floured surface to a round, 5 mm (¼ inch) thick. Place the loose bottom of the flan tin on the dough and trim the pastry round it to fit. Slide the loose bottom under the pastry round and place both in the tin. Gently press the pastry to the side of the tin, keeping the surface level. Spread with the conserve, leaving a 2.5 cm (1 inch) border round the edge.

Gather the dough trimmings together and roll out to a 3 mm (⅛ inch) thickness, then cut into strips 1 cm (½ inch) wide and long enough to fit across the flan and form a lattice pattern over the jam. Shape the remaining dough into a rope to fit neatly round the edge and flatten in position with a fork, forming a low, serrated edge.

Bake in a preheated moderately hot oven, 190°C (375°F), Gas Mark 5, for 30 minutes or until golden. Leave until cool, then brush with the warm apricot jam.
Makes one 23 cm (9 inch) tart

Linzer Lemon Tarts

LINZER PASTRY:
125 g (4 oz) butter
175 g (6 oz) icing
   sugar, sifted
1 egg, beaten
finely grated rind of
   1 lemon
125 g (4 oz) ground
   almonds
125 g (4 oz) plain
   flour, sifted
FILLING:
350 g (12 oz) lemon
   curd

Make and chill the pastry as for Linzer Torten (opposite). Use to line thirty-six 6 cm (2½ inch) tartlet tins as follows: break off a piece of dough about the size of a walnut, place in the tartlet tin and press out to shape with the fingers; trim off the excess pastry with a knife to neaten the edge.

Place a good teaspoonful of lemon curd into each tartlet – do not overfill.

Bake in a preheated moderately hot oven, 190°C (375°F), Gas Mark 5, for 20 minutes, or until golden. Leave in the tins to cool slightly, then transfer to a wire rack.
Makes 36

Custard Pie

25 g (1 oz) butter
25 g (1 oz) plain
  flour
150 ml (¼ pint)
  milk
125 g (4 oz) sugar
1 egg yolk
1 tablespoon rum or
  brandy
caster sugar for
  sprinkling
PASTRY:
175 g (6 oz) plain
  flour, sifted
75 g (3 oz) butter,
  softened
75 g (3 oz) icing
  sugar, sifted
finely grated rind of
  1 lemon
1 egg

Melt the butter in a pan, stir in the
flour and cook, stirring, for
2 minutes to form a roux.

Gradually add the milk to make a
thick smooth sauce, then stir in the
sugar and bring back to the boil,
stirring constantly. Remove from the
heat and leave for 1 minute, then
whisk in the egg yolk and rum or
brandy. Leave to cool while making
the pastry.

Put all the pastry ingredients in a
bowl and mix together to form a soft
dough. Turn onto a well floured
surface and cut off one third for the
lid. Shape both pieces into thick
rounds and chill for 1 hour.

Lightly butter a loose-bottomed
18 cm (7 inch) cake tin and remove
the bottom. Take the larger piece of
dough and place it on the loose
bottom of the tin. Roll it out so that
it covers it neatly, then drop this
pastry-covered base back into the tin.
Using the backs of your fingers,
press the pastry out to form a well
about 2.5 cm (1 inch) high and 5 mm
(¼ inch) thick all the way round the
tin.

Turn the custard into the pastry
case, smoothing the top. Using a
palette knife, carefully pull the top
edge of pastry inwards onto the
custard so that it partly encloses it,
leaving a 13 cm (5 inch) circle of
uncovered custard in the middle.

Roll out the remaining pastry to a
15 cm (6 inch) round and use to
cover the custard. Using a fork, push
the edges of the pastry together.
Sprinkle liberally with caster sugar.

Bake in a preheated moderate
oven, 180°C (350°F), Gas Mark 4, for
45 minutes, until golden. Serve warm,
with cream and stewed plums if liked.

Serves 6

Galette Breton

3 egg yolks
175 g (6 oz) plain
  flour, sifted
200 g (7 oz) caster
  sugar
200 g (7 oz)
  unsalted butter
1 tablespoon rum

Reserve a little of the egg yolk for glazing. Put the rest with the remaining ingredients in a bowl and work together to form a smooth, pliable dough. Shape it into a flattened ball, wrap in cling film and chill for 1 hour.

Turn the dough onto a floured surface, knead lightly and roll out to fit a buttered, loose-bottomed, shallow 20 cm (8 inch) cake tin or flan tin. Lift it carefully into the tin and press gently to fit snugly.

Brush the surface with the reserved egg yolk then, using a fork, make a criss-cross pattern on the surface. Bake in a preheated moderate oven, 180°C (350°F), Gas Mark 4, for 25 minutes until golden. Cool on a wire rack.

Makes one 20 cm (8 inch) cake

YEAST BREADS & BAKES

Herb Bread

This bread is delicious toasted and served with pâté. The herbs can be varied to taste.

25 g (1 oz) fresh yeast
250 ml (8 fl oz) warm milk
1 egg, beaten
2 teaspoons dried tarragon
2 teaspoons sugar
2 teaspoons salt
350 g (12 oz) plain strong white flour, sifted
1 tablespoon oil
2 teaspoons fennel seed to garnish

Cream the yeast with half the milk. Put the remaining milk in a large bowl and mix in the egg, tarragon, sugar and salt. Add the yeast mixture and 300 g (10 oz) of the flour. Beat well to form a soft creamy dough. Add the remaining flour and the oil and beat until thoroughly blended.

Place the mixture in a well greased 500 g (1 lb) loaf tin, brush with water and sprinkle liberally with fennel seed. Cover with cling film and leave to rise in a warm place for 30 minutes.

Bake in a preheated moderately hot oven, 200°C (400°F), Gas Mark 6, for 25 to 30 minutes until golden brown and the bread sounds hollow when tapped. Cool on a wire rack.
Makes one 500 g (1 lb) loaf

Scones with Yeast

25 g (1 oz) fresh yeast
150 ml (¼ pint) warm water
625 g (1¼ lb) plain strong white flour
2 tablespoons baking powder
75 g (3 oz) butter
1 egg
125 g (4 oz) sugar
150 ml (¼ pint) milk
125 g (4 oz) sultanas
milk to glaze

Mix the yeast with the warm water and 50 g (2 oz) of the flour in a bowl; leave in a warm place for 30 minutes.

Sift remaining flour and the baking powder into a bowl and rub in the butter. Beat together the egg, sugar and milk and add to the flour with the yeast mixture. Mix vigorously to a smooth dough. Knead in the sultanas.

Knead and shape the dough into a ball. Turn onto a floured surface and roll out to 2.5 cm (1 inch) thickness. Cut into rounds with a 5 cm (2 inch) pastry cutter and place on a greased baking sheet. Cover with cling film and leave to rise for 40 minutes; brush with milk after 30 minutes.

Bake in a preheated hot oven, 230°C (450°F), Gas Mark 8, for 12 to 15 minutes. Cool on a wire rack.

Makes about 20

Devonshire Splits

BASIC PLAIN
  DOUGH:
25 g (1 oz) fresh
  yeast
225 ml (7½ fl oz)
  warm water
1 egg, beaten
75 g (3 oz) sugar
500 g (1 lb) plain
  strong white flour
½ teaspoon salt
50 g (2 oz) butter,
  softened
FILLING:
125 g (4 oz)
  raspberry jam
284 ml (½ pint)
  double cream,
  whipped
TO FINISH:
icing sugar, sifted,
  for sprinkling

Cream the yeast with the water, then beat in the egg, 1 teaspoon sugar and 4 tablespoons flour. Leave in a warm place for 30 minutes.

Sift remaining flour and the salt into a bowl. Make a well in the centre, add remaining sugar and yeast mixture and mix vigorously to a soft dough. Knead in the butter until the dough is smooth. Shape into a ball and place in a warmed lightly buttered bowl. Cover and leave to rise in a warm place for 30 minutes.

Cut the dough into 15 equal pieces and shape into balls. Leave for 5 minutes, then roll out on a floured surface into 10 cm (4 inch) rounds and fold in half. Place on warmed, greased baking sheets, cover and leave to rise in a warm place for 40 minutes.

Bake in a preheated hot oven, 220°C (425°F), Gas Mark 7, for 10 minutes. Cool on a wire rack. Pull apart at the fold and fill with jam and cream. Dust lightly with icing sugar.
Makes 15

70

Chelsea Buns

BASIC PLAIN DOUGH:
25 g (1 oz) fresh yeast
225 ml (7½ fl oz) warm water
1 egg, beaten
75 g (3 oz) sugar
500 g (1 lb) plain strong white flour
½ teaspoon salt
50 g (2 oz) butter, softened

FILLING:
150 g (5 oz) butter, melted
75 g (3 oz) sugar
125 g (4 oz) sultanas
1 teaspoon ground mixed spice

TO FINISH:
25 g (1 oz) caster sugar

Make up the dough and leave to rise as for Devonshire Splits (opposite).

Roll the dough out on a floured surface to a 45 × 30 cm (18 × 12 inch) rectangle. Cover with 125 g (4 oz) of the melted butter, leaving a 2.5 cm (1 inch) border on one long side; brush this with water.

Sprinkle the sugar, sultanas and spice over the buttery surface and roll up like a Swiss roll, sealing well along the dampened edge. Coat the roll with the remaining melted butter and cut into 1.5 cm (¾ inch) slices. Place in a greased baking tin, about 1 cm (½ inch) apart. Cover with cling film and leave to rise in a warm place for 40 minutes; they will spread until touching each other.

Bake in a preheated hot oven, 220°C (425°F), Gas Mark 7, for 12 to 15 minutes. Sprinkle with caster sugar, then transfer to a wire rack to cool.

Makes approximately 20

Butter Triangles

BASIC PLAIN
  DOUGH:
25 g (1 oz) fresh
  yeast
225 ml (7½ fl oz)
  warm water
1 egg, beaten
75 g (3 oz) sugar
500 g (1 lb) plain
  strong white flour
½ teaspoon salt
50 g (2 oz) butter,
  softened
FILLING:
125 g (4 oz) butter,
  melted
125 g (4 oz) lemon
  curd
TO FINISH:
beaten egg
50 g (2 oz) caster
  sugar

Make up the dough and leave to rise as for Devonshire Splits (see page 70).

Cut the dough into 15 equal pieces, knead lightly and shape into round balls. Cover with cling film and leave to 'rest' for 5 minutes, then roll out on a floured surface into 10 cm (4 inch) rounds. Brush with melted butter and place ½ teaspoon lemon curd in the centre of each round. Fold in half to make a semi-circle, brush with butter and fold again to make a quarter circle. Place on a warmed, greased baking sheet, brush with beaten egg and sprinkle with sugar. Leave to rise in a warm place for 20 to 25 minutes.

Bake in a preheated hot oven, 220°C (425°F), Gas Mark 7, for 10 minutes. Cool on a wire rack.
Makes 15

Lardy Cake

500 g (1 lb) plain
  strong white flour
1 teaspoon salt
150 g (5 oz) lard
50 g (2 oz)
  granulated sugar
300 ml (½ pint)
  warm milk
25 g (1 oz) fresh
  yeast
250 g (8 oz) currants
125 g (4 oz)
  sultanas
125 g (4 oz) soft
  brown sugar
1 teaspoon ground
  mixed spice

Sift the flour and salt into a bowl and
rub in 25 g (1 oz) of the lard; make a
well in the centre. Cream together
the granulated sugar, milk and yeast,
pour into the well and mix vigorously
to a smooth dough. Shape into a ball,
cover with cling film and leave to
rise in a warm place for 30 minutes.
Knead in the currants and sultanas,
cover and leave for 10 minutes.

Roll out on a floured surface to a
45 ×15 cm (18 × 6 inch) rectangle.
Soften remaining lard and spread
over top two thirds of the dough.
Sprinkle the brown sugar and spice
on top. Fold up the bottom third,
then fold the top third down. Roll
out to original size and roll up like a
Swiss roll. Cut in half and place each
piece cut-side up in a greased 15 cm
(6 inch) cake tin. Cover and leave in
a warm place for about 1 hour.

Bake in a preheated hot oven, 220°C
(425°F), Gas Mark 7, for 30 minutes.
Turn out immediately onto plates,
allowing any fat to run over the cakes.
Makes two 15 cm (6 inch) cakes

Bara Brith

The translation of bara brith is 'speckled bread'. This traditional Welsh loaf can be any shape or size.

250 g (8 oz) currants
150 g (5 oz) sultanas
25 g (1 oz) cut mixed peel
300 g (10 oz) plain strong white flour
1 teaspoon salt
15 g (½ oz) lard
25 g (1 oz) sugar
½ teaspoon ground mixed spice
1 egg
150 ml (¼ pint) warm milk
15 g (½ oz) fresh yeast
honey to glaze

Rinse the currants, sultanas and peel in warm water; drain and dry on kitchen paper. Sift the flour and salt into a bowl and rub in the lard; make a well in the centre. Mix the sugar and spice and turn into the well.

Beat together the egg and milk, add the yeast and stir until thoroughly blended. Leave in a warm place for 15 minutes. Pour onto the sugar and mix, drawing in the flour, to a smooth elastic dough.

Tear the fruit and peel into the dough until well incorporated; shape into a ball. Cover and leave for 10 minutes.

Shape the dough into a round and place on a greased baking sheet. Cover with cling film and leave to rise in a warm place for 1½ hours.

Bake in a preheated moderate oven, 180°C (350°F), Gas Mark 4, for 35 minutes, until golden. Turn onto a wire rack and brush with honey immediately.
Makes one loaf

Selkirk Bannock

250 g (8 oz) plain
  strong white flour
½ teaspoon salt
40 g (1½ oz) butter
40 g (1½ oz) sugar
150 ml (¼ pint)
  warm milk
15 g (½ oz) fresh
  yeast
250 g (8 oz)
  sultanas
beaten egg to glaze

Sift the flour and salt together into a mixing bowl and rub in the butter; make a well in the centre.

Dissolve the sugar in the milk, add the yeast and mix until thoroughly blended. Leave in a warm place for 15 minutes. Pour into the dry ingredients and mix vigorously for 5 minutes to a smooth dough.

Knead lightly and shape into a ball. Place in a warmed, lightly greased bowl, cover with cling film and leave to rise in a warm place for 30 minutes.

Tear in the sultanas until they are well distributed. Reshape the dough, cover and leave to rise for 15 minutes.

Shape into a ball, place on a warmed greased baking sheet, cover with cling film and leave to rise in a warm place for 1 hour. After 15 minutes flatten slightly; brush with beaten egg.

Bake in a preheated hot oven, 220°C (425°F), Gas Mark 7, for about 20 minutes, until golden. Cool on a wire rack.

Makes one bannock

Sally Lunns

RICH FERMENTED
   DOUGH:
*20 g (¾ oz) fresh
   yeast*
*150 ml (¼ pint)
   warm milk*
50 g (2 oz) sugar
*350 g (12 oz) plain
   strong white flour*
1 egg, beaten
*finely grated rind of
   1 lemon*
*50 g (2 oz) butter,
   softened*
beaten egg to glaze

Cream the yeast with the milk,
1 teaspoon sugar and 2 tablespoons
flour until smooth. Leave in a warm
place for 20 minutes.

Sift remaining flour into a bowl,
make a well in the centre and add the
remaining sugar, the egg, lemon rind,
and yeast mixture. Mix vigorously to
a smooth dough, add the butter and
mix well. Knead lightly and shape
into a ball. Place in a warm greased
bowl, cover with cling film and leave
to rise in a warm place for 30 minutes.

Divide the dough in half, shape
each piece into a ball and place in
2 warmed, greased 15 cm (6 inch)
round cake tins. Cover and leave to
rise in a warm place for 30 to
40 minutes, brushing with beaten
egg when half risen.

Bake in a preheated hot oven, 220°C
(425°F), Gas Mark 7, for 15 to 20 minutes or until golden brown. Transfer
to a wire rack to cool slightly. Serve
warm, spread with butter and jam.
Makes two 15 cm (6 inch) cakes

Bath Buns

*1 quantity rich
   fermented dough
   (see recipe)*
FILLING:
*125 g (4 oz)
   sultanas*
*thinly pared rind of
   2 lemons, shredded*
*50 g (2 oz) crushed
   cube sugar*
beaten egg to glaze

Make up the dough and leave to rise
as for Sally Lunns (above).

Sprinkle the sultanas, lemon rind
and half of the sugar onto the dough
in the bowl and tear in until well
distributed.

Shape roughly into 16 buns and
place on a warmed, buttered baking
sheet, spacing well apart. Cover and
leave to rise for about 20 minutes.
Brush lightly with beaten egg and
sprinkle with the remaining sugar.

Bake in a preheated hot oven,
230°C (450°F), Gas Mark 8, for 10 to
12 minutes until golden. Cool on a
wire rack.
Makes 16

Spicy Fruit Buns

1 egg
200 ml (⅓ pint)
    warm water
    (approximately)
75 g (3 oz) caster
    sugar
20 g (¾ oz) fresh
    yeast
550 g (1 lb 2 oz)
    plain strong white
    flour
1 teaspoon salt
3 teaspoons ground
    mixed spice
50 g (2 oz) lard
finely grated rind of
    1 lemon
50 g (2 oz) currants
50 g (2 oz) sultanas
25 g (1 oz) mixed
    peel
2 tablespoons golden
    syrup, warmed, to
    glaze

Beat the egg in a measuring jug and add water to make up to 300 ml (½ pint). Whisk in 2 teaspoons of the sugar, the yeast and 50 g (2 oz) of the flour, until smooth. Cover and leave in a warm place for 30 minutes.

Sift the remaining flour, salt and spice into a large bowl and rub in the lard. Make a well in the centre and add the remaining sugar, the lemon rind and yeast liquid. Gradually draw in the flour and mix to a smooth dough; mix in the fruit and peel. Shape the dough into a ball and place in a warmed lightly greased bowl. Cover with cling film and leave to rise in a warm place for 30 minutes.

Turn onto a floured surface and divide the dough into 12 pieces. Shape into balls and place on a warmed, greased baking sheet; flatten slightly. Cover with cling film and leave to rise in a warm place for 40 minutes.

Bake in a preheated hot oven, 230°C (450°F), Gas Mark 8, for 7 to 8 minutes. Brush the buns with syrup immediately; cool on a wire rack.
Makes 12

Pikelets

Buttered crumpets and pikelets must be two of the oldest teatime favourites, dating from the 17th century. They are similar, although pikelet batter is softer and pikelets are easier to cook, as crumpet rings are not needed.

20 g (¾ oz) fresh yeast
450 ml (¾ pint) warm water
350 g (12 oz) plain flour
1 teaspoon salt
¼ teaspoon bicarbonate of soda, blended with 2 tablespoons cold water
1 egg white, lightly whisked

Mix the yeast with the warm water in a large mixing bowl. Sift the flour and salt into the bowl and beat well until smooth. Cover with a cloth and leave in a warm place for 30 minutes or until the mixture rises and starts to drop. Mix in the blended bicarbonate, then fold in the egg white thoroughly, until smooth and the consistency of thick pouring cream.

Lightly grease a heavy-based pan and heat until a drop of batter sizzles immediately on contact. Drop tablespoonfuls of the batter into the pan and cook until the top is dry. Turn with a palette knife and cook the underside until lightly browned. Repeat with the remaining batter, making about 25 pikelets.

Serve immediately, or cool then toast lightly. Serve with butter.
Makes about 25

SAVOURY TREATS

Anchovy Whirls

1 × 50 g (1¾ oz)
  can anchovy
  fillets, drained
125 g (4 oz) pork
  sausage meat
125 g (4 oz) puff
  pastry*

Chop the anchovy fillets finely and mix with the sausage meat.

Roll out the pastry quite thinly on a floured surface to a rectangle, about 30 × 25 cm (12 × 10 inches), and prick well with a fork. Spread the sausage meat mixture over the pastry, to within 1 cm (½ inch) of the edges. Roll up like a Swiss roll from the long side to make a roll about 2.5 cm (1 inch) thick. Chill for 1 hour or until needed.

Cut the roll into slices 5 mm (¼ inch) thick and place 2.5cm (1 inch) apart on baking sheets. Bake in a preheated hot oven, 220°C (425°F), Gas Mark 7, for 15 minutes until golden. Serve warm or cold.

Makes 48

Pork and Garlic Bites

4 cloves garlic, finely
   chopped
250 g (8 oz) pork
   sausage meat
250 g (8 oz) puff
   pastry*
beaten egg to glaze

Mix the garlic and sausage meat together and form into four 30 cm (12 inch) lengths.

Roll out the pastry on a floured surface to a rectangle 30 × 25 cm (12 × 10 inches). Prick all over with a fork and dampen with water. Cut into 4 equal pieces, 30 cm (12 inches) long. Place a length of sausage meat along one edge of each piece and roll up in the pastry, enclosing it completely. Chill for 1 hour.

Brush the rolls with egg and cut into 3.5 cm (1½ inch) lengths. Place on a baking sheet and bake in a preheated hot oven, 220°C (425°F), Gas Mark 7, for 15 to 20 minutes, until golden. Serve warm or cold.
Makes 30

One-Bite Vol-au-Vents

175 g (6 oz) puff
  pastry*
beaten egg to glaze
ANCHOVY FILLING:
1 × 50 g (1¾ oz)
  can anchovy
  fillets, drained
mayonnaise
SPICY TOMATO
  FILLING:
1 quantity tomato
  filling (see page
  86)
Worcestershire or
  chilli sauce
PRAWN or SMOKED
  SALMON FILLING:
3 tablespoons
  mayonnaise
3 tablespoons double
  cream
lemon juice
chilli sauce
125 g (4 oz) small
  prawns, or smoked
  salmon, chopped

Roll out the pastry on a floured surface to a 5 mm (¼ inch) thickness. Cut out 30 rounds using a 5 cm (2 inch) pastry cutter and place 15 on a baking sheet. Using a 2.5 cm (1 inch) pastry cutter, remove the centres from the remaining rounds.

Prick the rounds on the baking sheet with a fork and brush lightly with water. Place the rings of pastry on top, pressing lightly together. Chill for 30 minutes.

Brush with beaten egg and bake in a preheated hot oven, 220°C (425°F), Gas Mark 7, for 15 to 20 minutes, until golden brown. If they rise and topple out of shape, push them back into position while baking. Leave to cool, then fill with one of the fillings.

Anchovy: Chop the anchovies finely and mix with mayonnaise to taste.

Spicy Tomato: Add Worcestershire or chilli sauce to taste to prepared tomato filling.

Prawn or smoked salmon: Mix the mayonnaise and cream with lemon juice and chilli sauce to taste. Add the prawns or salmon and mix well.

Makes 15

Gruyère Tarts

125 g (4 oz) crispy
  butter pastry*
FILLING:
75 g (3 oz) Gruyère
  cheese, finely
  grated
5 tablespoons double
  cream
1 egg, beaten
2 teaspoons kirsch
  (optional)
salt and pepper

Roll out the pastry very thinly on a floured surface and use to line twelve 6 cm (2½ inch) tartlet tins.

Mix the filling ingredients together, seasoning with salt and pepper to taste, and divide between the pastry cases.

Bake in a preheated hot oven, 220°C (425°F), Gas Mark 7, for 20 minutes, until golden. Serve warm.

Makes 12

VARIATION: Use Roquefort or Stilton cheese instead of Gruyère.

Eclairs Karoly

125 g (4 oz) choux
   pastry*
350 g (12 oz) smooth
   pâté

Spoon the choux pastry into a piping
bag, fitted with a 1cm (½ inch)
nozzle, and pipe into mounds the size
of half a walnut on dampened baking
sheets.

Bake in a preheated moderately hot
oven, 200°C (400°F), Gas Mark 6,
for 20 minutes, then lower the heat
to 180°C (350°F), Gas Mark 4, and
bake for a further 10 to 15 minutes,
until golden brown. Cool on a
wire rack.

Beat the pâté until soft and
creamy, then pipe or spoon a little
into each éclair.

Makes approximately 25

NOTE: The size of these is really a
matter of personal preference, but
they should not be larger than a
single mouthful.

Spinach and Cheese Pasties

350 g (12 oz) frozen
  chopped spinach,
  thawed and well
  drained
50 g (2 oz) cooked
  smoked ham, cut
  into 5 mm
  (¼ inch) dice
75 g (3 oz)
  Lancashire cheese
¼ teaspoon each salt
  and pepper
1 small egg, beaten
350 g (12 oz) puff
  pastry*
beaten egg to glaze

Mix the spinach and ham together in a bowl. Crumble the cheese into the bowl. Add the salt, pepper and egg and mix well. Chill until required.

Roll out the pastry on a floured surface to a 3 mm (⅛ inch) thickness and cut out about fifteen 10 cm (4 inch) circles. Roll each one across the centre to form an oval, thick at the ends and thinner in the middle; brush all over with water.

Place a heaped teaspoonful of the spinach filling in the centre of each round and fold the pastry over to form a half-moon shape; knock up and seal the edges firmly. Brush with beaten egg, place on a baking sheet and prick once with a fork. Chill for 30 minutes.

Bake in a preheated hot oven, 220°C (425°F), Gas Mark 7, for 15 minutes, until risen and golden. Transfer to a wire rack to cool slightly. Serve warm.

Makes about 15

Little Pizza Pies

150 g (6 oz) crispy
    butter pastry* or
    puff pastry*
75 g (3 oz) matured
    Cheddar cheese,
    grated
TOMATO FILLING:
15 g (½ oz) butter
125 g (4 oz) onion,
    thinly sliced
1 clove garlic, finely
    chopped
2 teaspoons tomato
    purée
1 × 397 g (14 oz)
    can tomatoes
1 teaspoon basil
pepper and sugar to
    taste
TO GARNISH:
6 black olives, stoned
    and halved
6 anchovy fillets,
    halved

First prepare the tomato filling. Melt
the butter in a frying pan, add the
onion and garlic and cook gently
until soft. Add the tomato purée.
Roughly chop the tomatoes and add
to the pan with their juice. Add the
basil and pepper and sugar to taste.

Simmer gently for about
30 minutes, until almost all of the
liquid has evaporated and the mixture
has thickened. Leave to cool.

Roll out the pastry thinly on a
floured surface and use to line twelve
6 cm (2½ inch) tartlet tins. Leave to
rest in the refrigerator for 30 minutes.
Place a heaped teaspoon of tomato
mixture in each pastry case and top
with cheese. Garnish with olive and
anchovy pieces.

Bake in a preheated moderately hot
oven, 200°C (400°F), Gas Mark 6, for
12 to 15 minutes or until the cheese
has melted and the pastry is lightly
browned. Serve warm.
Makes 12

Individual Quiches

175 g (6 oz) short
    flan pastry* or
    crispy butter
    pastry*
FILLING:
3 egg yolks
1 egg
salt and pepper
grated nutmeg
    (optional)
284 ml (½ pint)
    whipping or
    double cream
125 g (4 oz) leaf
    spinach, cooked,
    drained and chopped
150 g (5 oz) leeks,
    thinly sliced and
    softened in 15 g
    (½ oz) butter
125 g (4 oz) red
    peppers, finely
    diced and softened
    in 15 g (½ oz)
    butter

Roll out the pastry on a floured surface to a 3 mm (⅛ inch) thickness and use to line 12 straight-sided 6 cm (2½ inch) individual flan tins. Prick with a fork and chill for 1 hour. Bake 'blind' in a preheated moderately hot oven, 200°C (400°F), Gas Mark 6, for 15 minutes; removing the paper and beans after 12 minutes.

Meanwhile, prepare the filling. Whisk the egg yolks and the egg together, seasoning with salt, pepper and nutmeg, if using, to taste. Whisk in the cream and check the seasoning – it should be well seasoned.

Divide the mixture into three equal quantities. Mix one portion with the spinach, one portion with the leeks and one portion with the red peppers.

Spoon into the baked cases and return to the oven for 15 minutes, or until the filling is just firm to touch. Serve warm.

Makes 12

Creamy Leek Pasties

The flavour and appearance of the filling is improved if a high proportion of the green part of the leek is used.

350 g (12 oz) leeks,
  cut into 5 mm
  (¼ inch) slices
  and blanched in
  boiling water for
  2 minutes
142 ml (¼ pint)
  single cream
½ teaspoon salt
large pinch of white
  pepper
1 tablespoon plain
  flour, blended with
  2 tablespoons
  water
25 g (1 oz) butter
350 g (12 oz) puff
  pastry*
beaten egg to glaze

Drain the leeks and put in a saucepan with the cream, salt and pepper. Bring to the boil, then simmer for 5 minutes. Add the blended flour, stirring to form a thick creamy sauce. Allow to bubble gently for 1 minute, then remove from heat. Dot the butter over the top and set aside until cold.

Roll out the pastry on a floured surface to a 3 mm (⅛ inch) thickness and cut out about fifteen 10 cm (4 inch) circles. Roll each one across the centre to form an oval, thick at the ends and thinner in the middle; brush all over with water.

Place a tablespoonful of leek filling in the centre of each round and fold the pastry over to form a half-moon shape; seal edges firmly. Brush with egg, place on a baking sheet and prick once with a fork. Chill for 30 minutes.

Bake in a preheated hot oven, 220°C (425°F), Gas Mark 7, for 15 minutes, until risen and golden. Transfer to a wire rack to cool slightly. Serve warm.
Makes about 15

Cheese and Onion Tartlets

250 g (8 oz) short
  flan pastry* or
  crispy butter
  pastry*
150 g (5 oz) onion,
  chopped
6 tablespoons milk
salt and pepper
275 g (9 oz)
  Lancashire cheese,
  grated
1 small egg, beaten

Roll out the pastry thinly on a floured surface and use to line about twenty 6 cm (2½ inch) tartlet tins.

Place the onion in a saucepan, add the milk, and salt and pepper to taste. Bring to the boil, then simmer for 1 minute. Remove from heat and stir in the cheese and egg. Leave until cold, then spoon into the pastry cases.

Bake in a preheated moderately hot oven, 200°C (400°F), Gas Mark 6, for 15 minutes until golden. Serve warm.
Makes about 20

BASIC RECIPES

Sweet Short Pastry

200 g (7 oz) butter,
  softened
1 tablespoon icing
  sugar, sifted
1 egg
1 tablespoon water
350 g (12 oz) plain
  flour, sifted

Mix the butter and icing sugar together until soft and creamy. Mix the egg and water together and gradually add to the butter. Add the flour and mix with a knife to a smooth dough.

Wrap in cling film and chill for 1 hour. Use as required.
Makes a 350 g (12 oz) quantity

Short Flan Pastry

This pastry is rich and short, easy to work with and does not shrink or go out of shape during baking – ideal when shape and appearance are important.

1 egg
1/2 teaspoon salt
150 g (5 oz) butter,
  softened
250 g (8 oz) plain
  flour, sifted

Whisk the egg and salt together, then mix into the butter a little at a time. Add the flour and mix to a smooth dough. Wrap in cling film and chill for 15 minutes.

Use as required.
Makes a 250 g (8 oz) quantity

Crispy Butter Pastry

This pastry is rich and short, with a crisp eating quality. It does tend to distort and shrink a little during baking, so make sure it has plenty of 'rest' before baking.

250 g (8 oz) plain
  flour
1/2 teaspoon salt
150 g (6 oz) butter,
  chilled and cut into
  1 cm (1/2 inch)
  cubes
4 tablespoons water
  (approximately)

Sift the flour and salt into a bowl and rub in the butter until the mixture resembles breadcrumbs. Add the water gradually and mix to a smooth dough. Wrap in cling film and chill for 30 minutes. Use as required.
Makes a 250 g (8 oz) quantity
NOTE: The butter must be well chilled, otherwise the mixture becomes too sticky. This pastry is rather soft to handle, so keep it very cold to work with.

Easy Flaky Pastry

350 g (12 oz) plain
    flour
50 g (2 oz) lard
175 g (6 oz) butter,
    chilled and cut into
    5 mm (¼ inch)
    dice
6 tablespoons water

Sift the flour into a bowl and rub in the lard. Add the diced butter and rub in until the mixture resembles breadcrumbs. Sprinkle on the water and mix with a knife to a smooth dough. Turn onto a floured surface and shape into a flat disc. Wrap in cling film and chill for 1 hour. Use as required.

Makes a 350 g (12 oz) quantity

NOTE: Everything for this recipe must be cold so that the butter is distributed in tiny particles throughout the pastry.

Puff Pastry

350 g (12 oz) plain
    flour
½ teaspoon salt
350 g (12 oz) butter,
    chilled
175 ml (6 fl oz) iced
    water

Sift the flour and salt into a bowl and rub in 50 g (2 oz) of the butter. Gradually add the water and mix to a smooth, stiff dough. Wrap in cling film and chill for 30 minutes.

Roll out on a floured surface to a rectangle 38 × 20 cm (15 × 8 inches). Cut the remaining butter into slices about 5 mm (¼ inch) thick and use to cover top two thirds of the dough. Fold the uncovered dough up over half the buttered dough, then fold the remaining buttered dough down on top, forming 3 layers of dough.

Roll out again to approximately 50 × 20 cm (20 × 8 inches). Fold the top third down, then fold the bottom third over the top. Wrap in cling film and chill for 1 hour.

Repeat this process 4 more times, giving the dough a quarter turn before rolling each time; chill for 1 hour after the first two times and 2 hours after the final two. Use as required.

Makes a 350 g (12 oz) quantity

NOTE: Frozen puff pastry is very good and can be used if you don't have time to make your own.

Choux Pastry

65 g (2½ oz) butter
175 ml (6 fl oz)
  water
1 level teaspoon
  sugar
100 g (3½ oz) plain
  flour
3 size 1 eggs, beaten

Place the butter, water and sugar in a saucepan and bring to the boil. Add the flour and beat well over a medium heat for 3 minutes, until the mixture forms a soft, smooth dough and leaves the side of the pan.

Tip the hot dough into a large basin and beat in the eggs a little at a time, beating well after each addition. Add the last egg gradually – the mixture should be soft but stiff enough to hold its shape when dropped off the spoon. Continue beating until the dough is smooth and glossy. Use as required.

Makes a 125 g (4 oz) quantity

Crème Pâtissière

7 egg yolks
175 g (6 oz) caster
  sugar
40 g (1½ oz) plain
  flour, sifted
vanilla essence
600 ml (1 pint) milk
25 g (1 oz) unsalted
  butter

Whisk together the egg yolks, sugar, flour and vanilla essence to taste until the mixture is light.

Bring the milk to the boil in a heavy-based pan, then pour it onto the egg mixture, whisking constantly. Return to the pan and whisk vigorously, over high heat until thickened; do not let it boil – lift the pan off and on the heat to control the thickening.

Turn the custard into a clean dry bowl and dot the butter over the surface to melt and prevent a skin from forming. Cool, then stir to incorporate the butter. Use as required.

Makes a 600 ml (1 pint) quantity

Swiss Buttercream

250 g (8 oz)
  unsalted butter,
  softened
3 size 3 or 4 size 6
  eggs
250 g (8 oz) caster
  sugar

Beat the butter until light. Whisk the eggs and sugar together for about 10 minutes until pale and thick, using an electric beater if possible.
Gradually add to the butter a little at a time, whisking constantly.
Continue whisking until the cream is light and smooth. Add flavouring if required.
This quantity is sufficient to fill and cover a 23 cm (9 inch) sandwich cake.
NOTE: It is essential that all of the ingredients are at room temperature before mixing otherwise the mixture will curdle.

Sugar Syrup

150 ml (¼ pint)
  water
125 g (4 oz) sugar

Put the water and sugar in a saucepan and heat gently until dissolved. Bring to a rolling boil. Boil for 1 minute, remove from the heat and cool.
Flavour with any liqueur or spirit to whatever strength desired.
This quantity is sufficient to soak one 23 cm (9 inch) sandwich cake

Ganache

120 ml (4 fl oz)
  single cream
250 g (8 oz) plain
  chocolate, grated
rum, brandy or
  liqueur (optional)

Put the cream in a heavy-based saucepan and bring to the boil. Stir in the chocolate. Remove from the heat and stir until well blended. Add spirit or liqueur to taste, if using. Leave in a cool place until suitable for spreading, then use as required.
If the ganache separates when being mixed, warm it slightly or add a little warm chocolate.
Serve warm as a chocolate sauce; beat until light and use as a cake filling or topping; or blend with buttercream to flavour.
This quantity is sufficient to coat one Sacher Torte

INDEX

Acknowledgments

Photography by Roger Phillips
Food prepared by Jane Suthering and Carole Handslip
Photographic stylist: Penny Markham